D0997077

GRAPHIS PHOTO 88

GRAPHIS PHOTO 88

The International Annual of Photography
Das Internationale Jahrbuch der Photographie
Le Répertoire International de la Photographie

Edited by/Herausgegeben von/Réalisé par
B. Martin Pedersen

Publisher and Creative Director: B. Martin Pedersen
Assistant Editors: Annette Crandall, Heinke Jenssen
Designers: Marino Bianchera, Martin Byland
Photographer: Walter Zuber

Graphis Press Corp., Zurich (Switzerland)

GRAPHIS PUBLICATIONS

GRAPHIS, International bi-monthly journal of graphic art and photography
GRAPHIS DESIGN ANNUAL, The international annual on design and illustration
GRAPHIS PHOTO, The international annual of photography
GRAPHIS POSTER, The international annual of poster art
GRAPHIS PACKAGING VOL. 5, An international survey of packaging design
GRAPHIS DIAGRAMS VOL. 2, The graphic visualization of abstract, technical and statistical facts and functions
GRAPHIS COVERS, An anthology of all GRAPHIS covers from 1944-86 with artists' short biographies
    and indexes of all GRAPHIS issues
GRAPHIS ANNUAL REPORTS, An international compilation of the best designed annual reports
FILM + TV GRAPHICS 2, An international survey of the art of film animation

GRAPHIS-PUBLIKATIONEN

GRAPHIS, Die internationale Zweimonatszeitschrift für Graphik und Photographie
GRAPHIS DESIGN ANNUAL, Das internationale Jahrbuch über Design und Illustration
GRAPHIS PHOTO, Das internationale Jahrbuch der Photographie
GRAPHIS POSTER, Das internationale Jahrbuch der Plakatkunst
GRAPHIS PACKUNGEN BAND 5, Internationaler Überblick der Packungsgestaltung
GRAPHIS DIAGRAMS BAND 2, Die graphische Darstellung abstrakter, technischer und statistischer Daten und Fakten
GRAPHIS COVERS, Eine Sammlung aller GRAPHIS-Umschläge von 1944-86 mit Informationen über die Künstler
    und Inhaltsübersichten aller Ausgaben der Zeitschrift GRAPHIS
GRAPHIS ANNUAL REPORTS, Ein internationaler Überblick der Gestaltung von Jahresberichten
FILM + TV GRAPHICS 2, Ein internationaler Überblick über die Kunst des Animationsfilms

PUBLICATIONS GRAPHIS

GRAPHIS, La revue bimestrielle internationale d'arts graphiques et de la photographie
GRAPHIS ANNUAL, Le répertoire international de la communication visuelle
GRAPHIS PHOTO, Le répertoire international de la photographie
GRAPHIS POSTER, Le répertoire international de l'art de l'affiche
GRAPHIS EMBALLAGES VOL. 5, Répertoire international des formes de l'emballage
GRAPHIS DIAGRAMS VOL. 2, La représentation graphique de faits et donnés abstraits, techniques et statistiques
GRAPHIS COVERS, Recueil de toutes les couvertures de GRAPHIS de 1944-86 avec des notices biographiques
    des artistes et le sommaire de tous les numéros du magazine GRAPHIS.
GRAPHIS ANNUAL REPORTS, Panorama international du design de rapports annuels d'entreprises
FILM + TV GRAPHICS 2, Un panorama international de l'art du film d'animation

PUBLICATION No. 189 (ISBN 3-85709-288-2)
© Copyright under Universal Copyright Convention
Copyright 1987 by Graphis Press Corp., 107 Dufourstrasse, 8008 Zurich, Switzerland
No part of this book may be reproduced in any form without written permission of the publisher
Printed in Japan by Toppan
Typeset in Switzerland by Setzerei Heller, Zurich
Typefaces: Garamond ITC Light Condensed, Futura Extra Bold

ABBREVIATIONS

Australia	AUS
Austria	AUT
Belgium	BEL
Canada	CAN
Denmark	DEN
France	FRA
Germany (West)	GER
Great Britain	GBR
Hong Kong	HKG
Ireland	IRL
Italy	ITA
Japan	JPN
Netherlands	NLD
Norway	NOR
Singapore	SIN
Spain	SPA
Sweden	SWE
Switzerland	SWI
USA	USA

ABKÜRZUNGEN

Australien	AUS
Belgien	BEL
Dänemark	DEN
Deutschland (BRD)	GER
Frankreich	FRA
Grossbritannien	GBR
Hongkong	HKG
Irland	IRL
Italien	ITA
Japan	JPN
Kanada	CAN
Niederlande	NLD
Norwegen	NOR
Österreich	AUT
Schweden	SWE
Schweiz	SWI
Singapur	SIN
Spanien	SPA
USA	USA

ABRÉVIATIONS

Allemagne occidentale	GER
Australie	AUS
Autriche	AUT
Belgique	BEL
Canada	CAN
Danemark	DEN
Espagne	SPA
Etats-Unis	USA
France	FRA
Grande-Bretagne	GBR
Hongkong	HKG
Irlande	IRL
Italie	ITA
Japon	JPN
Norvège	NOR
Pays-Bas	NLD
Singapour	SIN
Suède	SWE
Suisse	SWI

REMARKS

■ Our sincere thanks are extended to all photographers and to everyone who contributed – directly or indirectly – to this international annual of photography.

■ Entry instructions may be requested at:
Graphis Press Corp., Dufourstrasse 107,
8008 Zurich, Switzerland

ANMERKUNGEN

■ Unser herzlicher Dank gilt allen Photographen und Einsendern, die direkt oder indirekt zu diesem internationalen Jahrbuch der Photographie beigetragen haben.

■ Teilnahmebedingungen:
Graphis Verlag AG, Dufourstrasse 107,
8008 Zurich, Schweiz

AVERTISSEMENT

■ Nos remerciements vont à tous les photographes et collaborateurs qui ont apporté leur contribution directe ou indirecte au présent annuel international de photographie.

■ Demande de participation:
Editions Graphis SA, Dufourstrasse 107,
8008 Zurich, Suisse

One picture says more than a thousand words, that's how the saying goes. So what do you reckon 394 pictures say? That's how many there are in this volume of GRAPHIS PHOTO 88. How many words then do they constitute, consider and convey?

As a journalist I'm in a position where I have to assert myself day in, day out – with verbs versus visuals. And it's not so easy since the picture makers are holding all the tougher-argument cards in their decks. We'd all much rather take a look at a picture than have to wade through a thousand words!

And nearly all newsprint producers use this to advantage. An average newspaper page contains a few thousand words – plus one or two illustrations. But it's those few photos that stand out way in front of all that gray stuff. Pictures are not only a better eye-catcher, but they stick longer in the memory too.

Communications research can clearly prove that a written text in a newspaper or magazine is far more likely to be read if it's accompanied by an illustration. In other words it's the picture that is the attraction. Sure, there are exceptions. There is the *Neue Zürcher Zeitung* for instance. And *Le Monde.* And there is the *Financial Times* too. They're word-sheets who believe that even now they can do without these visual attractions. Pictures in their text columns are hardly the size of postage stamps. Generous illustrations appear – characteristically – in the advertisements, but, like I said, there are exceptions. Because of their uniqueness and their special function these newspapers till now have been able to stave off the competition by the tabloids, magazines and television, and I guess they'll continue to do so. But if you follow these papers' development closely over the years, you'll realize too that the postage stamps have been gradually getting bigger.

Dominating the world of the press are those products that take advantage of the appeal of the visual as medium. Understandably. Communications studies can prove that an indecisive customer at the newsvendor's stand makes up his mind to buy a certain magazine in the space of four or five seconds. And the picture is much better suited for influencing snap decisions like this, than a whole heap of words.

Yes, we've got headlines to beat the big drum for us too. But reality in a straight-to-the-point headline can only be condensed in monosyllabic form – and frequently has to knuckle under for the sake of a tight-knit sensational headline to the extent that it is even misrepresented. (We won't talk about the intentional falsifying.) A picture though is able to unite both sides; a picture can express total reality and yet appear sensational through the use of eye-popping elements – sensational in the true meaning of the word: stimulating the senses.

We remember pictures easily. That photo of the burning "Hindenburg" at Lakehurst, the photograph of the small boy with uplifted hands in the ghetto of Warsaw, being transported at gunpoint by German soldiers; the photo of the Vietnamese girl fleeing from her Napalm-burnt native village – these photographs went round the world. They were nailed to our memory with a sledge-hammer. But which of us remembers the words that accompanied them?

And picture-stills from the movies have even more effect than the printed ones. Whose feelings were not rent in Sergei Eisenstein classic *Battleship Potemkin* when the baby's pram rolled down the steps – and straight into our hearts? Who can remember any more of the film though? The film-still of the airport of Casablanca, where Humphrey Bogart takes leave – physically and emotionally – of Ingrid Bergman in the fog it remains a classic and will continue to be adapted for all kinds of new purposes. The words that belong to it, however, are dead and buried, without very much loss.

The most sophisticated "picture" makers are without doubt the advertisers, for they have created, from their original handiwork, a contemporary photoart. The Marlboro Cowboy sells his cigarettes – but not because of his great oration.

"In the beginning was the Word," so it says in the best known book with the greatest circulation of all time. This book developed into an impressive power of persuasion only with its words. But that happened mainly at a time when pictures were not so prevalent. Now, when we see the daily world news on television, travel catalogs, video cassettes, and advertising posters, the words in the good book are having a hard time of it.

Ever since the picture started out on its triumphant march the word in general is having to battle hard. Admittedly from time to time there are great words spoken: "To be or not to be, that is the question." William Shakespeare put these words on the lips of his Hamlet four hundred years ago. And this simple sentence, a headline in its strength and effect, is envied by every writer. It has gone down in the annals of history – but only as an empty formula – as a word-sleeve. Who today puts this phrase in the context that Shakespeare gave it a few centuries ago? A picture such as *Liberty Leading the People* by Eugène Delacroix, on the other hand, painted at the beginning of the last century, brings the French Revolution right up front of the mind's eye instinctively. Even if the viewer has no strong feelings one way or the other about the French or any other revolution. This picture is doubtless less known than Hamlet's famous words.

Why pictures radiate such power over words is obvious when you look through GRAPHIS PHOTO 88: here are the best photographs by the best photographers. In this volume you can well appreciate that a good photo has at least as much content as a good written description. In other words: in a good picture there is much more than you can get on a scrap of celluloid measuring 24 x 36 millimeters. Behind this minute flimsy rectangle lies a long, long story – the story of the whole zeppelin air trip and the twenties era; the history of the Warsaw ghetto and its seizure and destruction by the Nazis, even Fascism in its totality; or the Vietnam war, if we think back to our examples.

These stories contain a lot more than only a thousand words, and while the picture doesn't tell all, it certainly tells a great many of them.

And there stands – much less dramatically – the marketing concept behind the selling of a product, plus the strategy of an ad agency that has to do this efficiently. And finally the most attractive and skilled translation by the photographer. All these mental preliminaries as well as the thousands of drafts, find themselves at last artistically composed – to come alive in the resulting picture. It is only appropriate that the small negative is duplicated a thousand times and blown up to poster size so that it can show all that is included in the picture.

It's obvious: as a man of words I envy those who are able to express themselves with photographs; who make their visual "language" so powerful that it triggers off all kinds of effects and emotions. But I am also absolutely convinced that both of these media are necessary; that the picture without the word has no chance. In the media business especially, this mutual dependence comes to light. The increased appeal of the written text through its related illustration is one aspect. The other is summarized in the old handcraft rulebook of journalism: "Every picture needs a caption."

For even if a picture alone says more than a thousand words, and to write a lot more about it would be superfluous and nonsensical, nevertheless, a few well-chosen words help every picture. This applies no less to GRAPHIS PHOTO 88. All the 394 pictures would be just as fascinating without the small explanatory text, but the short, additional piece of information assists the viewer in understanding them better. Obviously the "picture people" who designed this book were of the same opinion: a truly great picture needs a few restrained words just to keep the scales nicely balanced.

HEINI LÜTHY, born in 1954, is editor of the Swiss magazine Politik und Wirtschaft. As producer he is also largely responsible for the visual design of the magazine.

Ein Bild sagt mehr als tausend Worte, behauptet das Sprichwort. Was aber sagen dann erst 394 Bilder, so viele wie dieses GRAPHIS PHOTO 88 zeigt? Wie viele Worte wiegen sie auf?

Als Journalist bin ich in der Situation, dass ich mich tagtäglich mit geschriebenen Worten gegen die Bilder der Photographen und Illustratoren behaupten muss. Und es ist schwierig, denn offenbar haben die Bild-Macher die besseren, die stärkeren Argumente: Jedermann schaut lieber ein Bild an, als tausend Worte lesen zu müssen.

Dies machen sich heute fast alle Presseerzeugnisse zu Nutzen: Eine durchschnittliche Zeitungsseite enthält ein paar tausend Worte und ein, zwei Bilder, und die wenigen Bilder fallen bei weitem stärker auf als die vielen Worte, und dies in zweierlei Hinsicht: Sie sind nicht nur der bessere Blickfang im ersten Moment, sie bleiben auch länger im Gedächtnis haften.

Die Kommunikationsforschung kann heute klar beweisen, dass ein geschriebener Text in einer Zeitung oder Zeitschrift viel eher gelesen wird, wenn er entsprechend illustriert ist. Das heisst nichts anderes, als dass das Bild die Attraktion ist. Sicher, es gibt Ausnahmen, es gibt die *Neue Zürcher Zeitung*, es gibt *Le Monde*, es gibt die *Financial Times*, Wörter-Blätter, welche auch heute noch auf diese Attraktion glauben verzichten zu können; Bilder in den Textspalten erreichen höchstens die Grösse von Briefmarken, grosszügige Illustrationen kommen allenfalls in den Anzeigen vor - bezeichnenderweise. Aber wie gesagt, dies sind Ausnahmen; wegen ihrer Einzigartigkeit und ihrer besonderen Funktion haben sich diese Zeitungen bisher gegen die Konkurrenz von Boulevard-Presse, Magazinen und Fernsehen behauptet und werden dies auch weiterhin tun können. Aber wenn man ihre Entwicklung über Jahre verfolgt, so wird man gewahr, dass die Briefmarken allmählich grösser werden.

Dominierend in der Welt der Presse sind hingegen diejenigen Produkte, welche die Attraktivität des Mediums Bild ausnützen. Begreiflich: Die Kommunikationsforschung kann ebenfalls beweisen, dass sich ein unentschlossener Kunde am Kiosk innerhalb von Sekunden zum Kauf einer bestimmten Zeitschrift entscheidet. Und um innerhalb dieser kurzen Zeit möglichst grossen Eindruck auf den Unentschlossenen zu machen, eignet sich ein Bild viel besser als ein Haufen Worte.

Zwar gibt es auch Schlagzeilen. Doch die Wirklichkeit kann mit Schlagzeilen immer nur verkürzt wiedergegeben werden - manchmal wird sie um der Schlagzeile willen so stark verkürzt, dass die Wirklichkeit sogar verfälscht wird (von der absichtlichen Verfälschung soll hier nicht die Rede sein). Ein Bild hingegen kann beide Seiten miteinander vereinbaren, ein Bild kann gleichzeitig eine ganze Wirklichkeit ausdrücken und dennoch durch einige ganz wenige, ins Auge springende Elemente sensationell wirken, sensationell im wahren Sinne des Wortes: die Sinne erregend.

An Bilder erinnern wir uns leicht: An die Photographie der brennenden «Hindenburg» in Lakehurst, an das Bild des kleinen Jungen mit erhobenen Händen im Getto von Warschau, der von deutschen Soldaten mit vorgehaltenem Gewehr weggeführt wird, an das Bild des vietnamesischen Mädchens, das schreiend aus dem vom Napalm verbrannten Heimatdorf flieht - diese Bilder sind um die Welt gegangen, bleiben in der Erinnerung festgemeisselt. Wer aber erinnert sich an die Worte, die damals dazu geschrieben wurden?

Noch mehr als die gedruckten Bilder wirken die bewegten: Wem ist nicht der Kinderwagen, der in Sergeji Eisensteins Klassiker *Panzerkreuzer Potemkin* aus den zwanziger Jahren die Treppe herunterrollt, direkt ins Herz gefahren? Wer aber erinnert sich noch an den Film? Das Bild auf dem Flugplatz von Casablanca, als Humphrey Bogart sich von Ingrid Bergmann im Nebel - auch der Gefühle - verabschiedet, bleibt ein Klassiker und wird deshalb auch immer wieder aufgenommen und für neue Zwecke adaptiert. Die Worte aber, die dazugehören, sind der Weltgeschichte ohne Verlust verlorengegangen.

Die raffiniertesten Bilder-Macher sind ohne Zweifel die Werber: Sie haben aus ihrem ursprünglichen Handwerk eine eigentliche zeitgenössische Bilder-Kunst geschaffen. Der Marlboro-Cowboy verkauft seine Zigaretten bekanntlich nicht deswegen, weil er grosse Worte macht.

«Am Anfang war das Wort», heisst es zwar in der wohl bekanntesten und am weitesten verbreiteten Publikation der Welt, der Bibel. Diese hat als grosse Ausnahme – neben den erwähnten Zeitungen – allein mit Worten eine eindrucksvolle Überzeugungskraft entwickelt. Aber das war vor allem zu Zeiten, als das Bild noch nicht so weit verbreitet war; jetzt, im Zeitalter von Fernsehen, Reiseprospekten, Videokassetten und Werbeplakaten, hat es das Wort Gottes bekanntlich recht schwer.

Seit das Bild seinen Siegeszug angetreten hat, hat es das Wort schwer. Von Zeit zu Zeit werden grosse Worte ausgesprochen, mit «Sein oder Nichtsein, das ist hier die Frage», legte William Shakespeare seinem Hamlet vor vierhundert Jahren ein solches in den Mund. Und dieser einfache Satz, eine Schlagzeile, um deren Kraft und Wirkung jeder Journalist den Dichter beneiden muss, ist in die Geschichte eingegangen – aber nur als leere Formel, als Worthülse. Wer verbindet diesen Satz heute, vier Jahrhunderte später, noch mit dem Inhalt, den ihm Shakespeare damals gab? Ein Bild wie *Die Freiheit auf den Barrikaden* von Eugène Delacroix andererseits, gemalt Anfang des letzten Jahrhunderts, lässt vor dem geistigen Auge des Betrachters unwillkürlich die Französische Revolution auferstehen, auch wenn er zur Französischen oder irgendwelchen Revolutionen überhaupt keine Beziehung hat. Dabei sei nur am Rande erwähnt, dass das Bild zweifellos viel weniger Menschen bekannt ist als das Hamlet-Wort.

Warum Bilder gegenüber den Worten eine so grosse Kraft ausstrahlen, versteht man gerade beim Betrachten von GRAPHIS PHOTO 88 sehr gut, sind doch hier die besten Bilder der besten Photographen versammelt. Hier erkennt man: Ein gutes Bild hat mindestens ebensoviel Inhalt wie eine gute Beschreibung in Worten. Anders gesagt: in einem guten Bild steckt viel mehr, als sich auf einem Zelluloid-Rechteck von 24 mal 36 Millimeter unterbringen lässt. Dahinter steht in Wirklichkeit eine ganze Geschichte, die Geschichte der ganzen Zeppelin-Luftfahrt und der zwanziger Jahre, die Geschichte des Warschauer Gettos, seiner Eroberung und Zerstörung durch die Nationalsozialisten, letztlich des ganzen Faschismus, oder des Vietnamkriegs, um die oben beschriebenen Beispiele aufzunehmen. Diese Geschichten aber sind viel mehr als nur tausend Worte lang, und das Bild gibt nicht alle, aber viele dieser Worte in sich wieder.

Oder es steht – viel weniger dramatisch – ganz einfach die Marktstrategie dahinter, ein Produkt zu verkaufen, plus die Strategie einer Werbeagentur, dies effizient zu tun, und schliesslich die möglichst attraktive Umsetzung durch den Photographen. All diese gedanklichen Vorarbeiten – auch die Tausende von Vor-Worten – finden sich schliesslich kunstvoll komponiert und verschachtelt im Endresultat Bild wieder. Da ist es nur billig, dass das kleine Rechteck tausendfach vervielfältigt und auf Plakatgrösse gebracht wird, damit all das auch zur Geltung kommt, was in dem einen Bild steckt.

Es ist offensichtlich: Als Wort-Mensch beneide ich die Leute, die mit Bildern etwas ausdrücken können, die dieser «Sprache» mächtig sind und mit ihr Wirkungen auslösen können. Aber ich bin auch fest davon überzeugt, dass beide Medien notwendig sind, dass das Bild ganz ohne das Wort keine Chance hat. Gerade im Pressegeschäft kommt diese gegenseitige Abhängigkeit immer wieder gut zum Vorschein. Die Attraktivitätssteigerung des geschriebenen Texts durch die entsprechende Illustration ist die eine Seite. Die andere ist in der alten Handwerksregel des Journalismus zusammengefasst: Jedes Bild braucht eine Bildlegende.

Zwar: wenn ein Bild allein mehr sagt als tausend Worte, so ist es meist weder nötig noch sinnvoll, dazu auch noch viel zu schreiben, aber ein paar wenige ergänzende Worte tun wohl jedem Bild gut. Dies gilt auch hier im GRAPHIS PHOTO 88: All die 394 Bilder wären ohne kurze Erklärungstexte zwar genauso faszinierend, aber die knappen zusätzlichen Informationen lassen den Betrachter sie besser verstehen. Offensichtlich sind auch die Bild-Menschen, welche das Buch gestaltet haben, der Meinung, dass es zu einem grossartigen Bild ein paar wenige, nüchterne Worte braucht, damit das gegenseitige Verhältnis stimmt.

HEINI LÜTHY, geboren 1954, ist Redaktor des Schweizer Magazins Politik und Wirtschaft. Als Produzent ist er dort massgeblich für die optische Gestaltung verantwortlich.

Un proverbe veut qu'une image en dise plus que mille mots. Et les 394 images alors qui constituent ce GRAPHIS PHOTO 88? A quel volume énorme de mots se substituent-elles?

Le journaliste que je suis doit chaque jour lutter pied à pied, la plume à la main, contre l'assaut des images de photographes et d'illustrateurs. La tâche est ardue, car les faiseurs d'images disposent manifestement d'arguments plus incisifs, plus frappants. Qui ne préfère pas contempler une image plutôt que de devoir se farcir un texte de mille mots?

La presque totalité des publications de presse en tire aujourd'hui profit. En effet, une page de journal contient en moyenne quelques milliers de mots et une ou deux images; or, ces quelques images ont bien plus de poids que tous ces mots, et cela de deux manières: elles ont le pouvoir d'accrocher l'attention sur le moment, et elles occupent l'esprit bien plus longtemps.

La recherche en matière de communication peut aujourd'hui démontrer sans risque d'erreur qu'un texte de journal ou de magazine est d'autant plus lu qu'il comporte des illustrations, ce qui revient à dire que l'image constitue l'attraction. Il y a certes des exceptions à cette règle: il y a la *Neue Zürcher Zeitung,* il y a *Le Monde,* il y a le *Financial Times* – autant de quotidiens bourrés de mots qui pensent pouvoir se payer le luxe de renoncer aujourd'hui encore à cette attraction; les images placées dans les colonnes atteignent tout au plus le format de timbres-poste, les illustrations au grand format ne se trouvent que dans la partie publicitaire (et encore), et c'est là un fait marquant. Pourtant il s'agit d'exceptions; leur caractère exceptionnel et leur fonction particulière leur ont permis de résister victorieusement à la concurrence de la presse à sensation, des magazines et de la télévision et de continuer à se prétendre dans leur fief. Il est toutefois intéressant de noter qu'au fil des années les «timbres-poste» ont tendance à s'agrandir.

Les produits qui dominent la scène journalistique sont au contraire tous ceux qui tirent profit de l'attrait du média «image». Cela se comprend: la recherche en matière de communication est également à même de prouver qu'un client indécis va mettre quatre ou cinq secondes à se décider à acheter tel périodique plutôt qu'un autre. Ce qui emportera sa décision en un laps de temps aussi court, ce sera indiscutablement une image accrochante plutôt qu'un salmigondis de mots.

Il est vrai qu'il y a les manchettes. Pourtant, les manchettes ne restituent le réel qu'en réduction. Parfois même, le réel est réduit à tel point que la manchette en donne une idée fausse (nous ne parlerons pas ici de la falsification intentionnelle du réel à travers les titres de la Une). Une image par contre peut concilier les deux extrêmes en exprimant la totalité du réel et en faisant simultanément sensation grâce à quelques éléments percutants – sensation au sens propre du terme, «qui en appelle aux sens, qui les stimule».

Les images, on s'en souvient facilement. C'est ainsi qu'on évoque sans difficulté le zeppelin «Hindenburg» en feu au haut de son mât à Lakehurst, le petit garçon levant les mains devant les armes allemandes braquées sur lui au fond du ghetto de Varsovie, la fillette viêtnamienne échappant en hurlant à l'enfer du napalm qui déferle sur son village. De telles images ont fait le tour du monde, elles restent bloquées dans la mémoire. Mais qui se souvient du texte qui les accompagnait à l'époque où elles furent réalisées?

L'effet de l'image imprimée se potentialise dès que l'on passe aux images animées. Qui n'a pas reçu comme un coup au cœur l'image de la poussette qui dégringole l'escalier dans *Le Cuirassé «Potemkine»* de Sergueï Mikhaïlovitch Eisenstein, le grand classique des années 20? Mais qui se rappelle encore l'action du film? L'image de l'aérodrome de Casablanca où Humphrey Bogart fait ses adieux à Ingrid Bergman dans le brouillard – qui teinte aussi les sentiments des personnages – reste une scène classique constamment reprise et réadaptée pour de nouveaux usages. Les mots qui l'accompagnaient ont sombré dans les poubelles de l'Histoire sans grande perte pour l'humanité.

Les faiseurs d'images les plus astucieux, on les trouve sans conteste parmi les publicitaires. Ce sont bien eux qui ont fait d'un métier artisanal à ses débuts un véritable art de l'image contemporaine. Le cowboy à la Marlboro ne vend visiblement pas ses cigarettes en raison des paroles qu'il prononce.

«Au début était le Verbe», nous dit la publication la plus répandue à travers le monde et donc la mieux connue – la Bible. Celle-ci constitue avec les journaux précités la grande exception d'un texte dont l'effet résulte du pouvoir de conviction qu'ont les mots qui y sont employés. Cet effet date pourtant d'une époque où l'image ne s'était pas encore généralisée. La parole de Dieu a davantage de peine à s'imposer de nos jours face au journal télévisé, aux prospectus de voyage, aux cassettes vidéo et aux affiches publicitaires.

Les mots ont fort à faire depuis que l'image vole de victoire en victoire. De temps à autre, des paroles font tilt à travers les âges, ainsi la fameuse phrase «Être ou ne pas être, telle est la question» que William Shakespeare a mise dans la bouche de son Hamlet il y a 400 ans. Cette phrase si simple, ce slogan dont la puissance et l'impact font pâlir de jalousie les journalistes est entrée dans l'histoire – mais seulement en tant que phrase creuse, douille vidée de sa charge de poudre. Qui est encore capable de donner à cette phrase son sens d'il y a quatre siècles? Par contre, un tableau tel que *La Liberté guidant le peuple* d'Eugène Delacroix évoque encore aujourd'hui irrésistiblement la Révolution française, même pour qui ne s'intéresse aucunement à cette révolution ou à quelque autre que ce soit. Notons en passant que ce tableau est certainement connu de bien moins de personnes que ne l'est la citation de Hamlet.

C'est en parcourant GRAPHIS PHOTO 88 que l'on comprend le mieux le pouvoir suggestif qui habite l'image et dont les mots sont dépourvus. L'ouvrage réunit en effet les meilleures images des meilleurs photographes. Un constat s'impose: une image de qualité a un contenu au moins aussi éloquent qu'une bonne description rédigée en mots. Autrement dit, une image contient bien davantage qu'un texte inscrit dans un rectangle de celluloïd de 24 x 36 mm. C'est que l'image incarne toute une histoire, l'histoire du dirigeable et des années 20, l'histoire du ghetto de Varsovie, de sa conquête et de sa destruction par le national-socialisme, voire l'histoire du fascisme tout entier, ou celle de la guerre du Viêt-nam – pour ne reprendre que les exemples énumérés plus haut. Or, ces histoires comptent bien plus de mille mots, et l'image sait restituer une foule énorme de ces mots, sinon la totalité.

Ou alors il s'agit – de manière bien moins dramatique – tout simplement de stratégie du marché visant à vendre un produit, à quoi s'ajoute la stratégie d'une agence de publicité qui entend réaliser cette vente de manière efficace, et en fin de compte la transposition la plus attrayante possible par l'art du photographe. Tout ce travail mental préliminaire – y compris les milliers de mots préparatoires – aboutit finalement à une composition par l'image savamment orchestrée et imbriquée. Il est alors équitable de multiplier le petit rectangle par milliers en lui donnant le format d'une affiche pour rendre pleinement justice à tout ce qui s'exprime à travers une image.

Une chose est évidente: homme du mot, j'envie ceux qui savent s'exprimer à travers l'image, qui maîtrisent ce «langage» et le mettent en œuvre pour déclencher des sensations. Pourtant je reste convaincu de ce que les deux médias ne vont pas l'un sans l'autre, de ce que l'image seule, dépourvue du mot, n'a pas d'avenir. C'est précisément dans le domaine de la presse que s'affirme chaque jour davantage cette interdépendance. Augmenter l'attrait du texte au moyen d'une illustration qui colle à ce texte est un aspect de la question. L'autre se résume dans cette vieille règle artisanale du journalisme: à chaque image, il faut une légende.

Il est vrai que si l'image à elle seule en dit plus que mille mots, il ne sera ni nécessaire ni judicieux d'y ajouter un tas de mots. Pourtant, quelques mots bien choisis font du bien à toute image. C'est ce qui se vérifie aussi dans GRAPHIS PHOTO 88: toutes ces 394 images exerceraient certes la même fascination sans les brefs textes explicatifs qui les accompagnent, mais les quelques informations écrites qui y sont ajoutées aident sensiblement à la compréhension. Les hommes à images qui ont conçu ce volume sont manifestement du même avis: une image, aussi merveilleuse soit-elle, a besoin de quelques mots sobres et efficaces pour que l'équilibre s'installe à la fois dans ce qui est contemplé et dans le cerveau de celui qui la contemple.

HEINI LÜTHY, né en 1954, est membre de la rédaction du magazine suisse Politik und Wirtschaft. En sa qualité de réalisateur, il est pour une large part responsable de la conception visuelle.

FASHION

MODE

FASHION

MODE

PHOTOGRAPHER:
Danilo Frontini
CLIENT:
VOGUE ENFANTS
PUBLISHER:
Condé Nast S.A.
ART DIRECTOR:
Franz Hubscher
■ 1–5

■ 1-5 Photographs from an article on children's fashion in the special issue *Vogue Enfants*. Seven famous Italian fashion designers show their ideas for winter 87/88. (FRA)

■ 1-5 Aufnahmen aus einem Beitrag über Kindermode im Sonderheft *Vogue Enfants*. Sieben berühmte italienische Modeschöpfer zeigen ihre Ideen für den Winter 87/88. (FRA)

■ 1-5 Photos illustrant un article de modes enfantines dans le cahier spécial *Vogue Enfants*. Sept grands couturiers italiens y présentent leurs idées pour l'hiver 87/88. (FRA)

PHOTOGRAPHER:
KOTO BOLOFO
CLIENT:
L'UOMO
PUBLISHER:
CONDÉ NAST S.P.A.
ART DIRECTOR:
ARMANDO CHITOLINA
■ 6–12

■ 6–12 Photographs from a fashion feature in the Italian men's fashion magazine *L'Uomo*. This issue devotes its main topic to the cinema and film industry, and the fashions shown, entitled "Hollywoodland", were inspired by old Hollywood movies. (ITA)

■ 6–12 Aufnahmen aus einem Modebeitrag im italienischen Herrenmodemagazin *L'Uomo*. Die Filmbranche ist das dominierende Thema dieser Ausgabe, und die hier unter dem Titel «Hollywoodland» gezeigte Mode wurde offensichtlich von alten Hollywoodfilmen inspiriert. (ITA)

■ 6–12 D'un article de mode dans le magazine masculin italien *L'Uomo*. Le numéro est consacré presque exclusivement au cinéma, ce qui explique que les modes présentées ici sous le titre de «Hollywoodland» évoquent la garde-robe des vedettes des vieux films hollywoodiens. (ITA)

■ 13 Example of the photographs contained in a calendar produced in Vienna on the theme "Remembering the 19th Century". (GER)

■ 14 Photograph from a fashion feature in the magazine *Jill.* The landscape of the English county of Dorset serves as a frame for the photograph. (GBR)

■ 13 Beispiel der für einen Jahreskalender bestimmten Aufnahmen, die in Wien zu dem Thema »Erinnerung an das 19. Jahrhundert« entstanden. (GER)

■ 14 Aufnahme aus einem Modebeitrag in der Zeitschrift *Jill.* Die englische Landschaft Dorset diente als Rahmen für die Aufnahme. (GBR)

■ 13 Exemple des photos destinées à un calendrier annuel intitulé «Souvenirs du XIXe siècle». Toute la série a été réalisée à Vienne. (GER)

■ 14 Photo pour un article de mode paru dans le magazine *Jill.* C'est le comté anglais de Dorset qui a fourni le cadre de cette vue. (GBR)

PHOTOGRAPHER:
THOMAS LÜTTGE
CLIENT:
*MÜNCHENER GASWERKE,
BAYERNGAS*
ART DIRECTOR:
THOMAS LÜTTGE
AGENCY:
FP-WERBUNG, MÜNCHEN
◄■13

PHOTOGRAPHER:
ANDREW MACPHERSON
PUBLISHER:
EDITIONS A.G. PRESS
►■14

PHOTOGRAPHER:
*CHRISTIAN VON
ALVENSLEBEN*
CLIENT:
*MUSTANG BEKLEIDUNGS-
WERKE GMBH & CO.*
ART DIRECTOR:
EBERHARD RAPP
DESIGNER:
*EBERHARD RAPP/
PETRA MOCK*
AGENCY:
*LEONHARDT & KERN
WERBUNG GMBH*
■ 15–21

  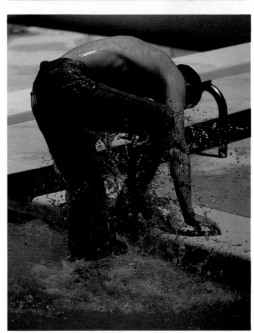

■ 15–21 Photographs from an advertising campaign for *Mustang* jeans. All photographs were shown full page. The titles are: *15* "Early Connection", *16* "Funny Lady", *17* "New Wave", *18* "Sea-Sun Season", *19* "Silent Skyline", *20* "Travellers Heaven" and *21* "Waterproof Cowboy". (GER)

■ 15–21 Aufnahmen aus einer Anzeigenkampagne für *Mustang*-Jeans. Alle Photos werden ganzseitig gezeigt. Ihre Titel lauten: *15* «Early Connection», *16* «Funny Lady», *17* «New Wave», *18* «Sea-Sun Season», *19* «Silent Skyline», *20* «Travellers Heaven» und *21* «Waterproof Cowboy». (GER)

■ 15–21 Photos tirées d'une campagne d'annonces en faveur des jeans *Mustang*. Elles sont intitulées: *15* «Correspondance rapide», *16* «P'tite Dame marrante», *17* «Nouvelle Vague», *18* «Saison mer-soleil», *19* «Skyline de silence», *20* «Paradis des voyageurs», *21* «Cowboy imperméable». (GER)

PHOTOGRAPHER:
Monika Robl
CLIENT:
Salko
ART DIRECTOR:
H. Edler
DESIGNER:
H. Edler
AGENCY:
MMS Werbeagentur
■ 22–24

PHOTOGRAPHER:
CONNY WINTER
CLIENT:
BREUNINGER
ART DIRECTOR:
CHARLES BARLOGIS
AGENCY:
BARLOGIS & JAGGI
■ 25

■ 22-24 Examples of the photographs from a catalog entitled "Classic Loden Collection" by *Salko,* Salzburg, Austria.
The setting is Fuschl Castle, built in the mid 15th century by
Archbishop Friedrich IV Truchsass von Emmerberg as a
country estate for his hunting guests. The castle has now
been turned into a luxury hotel. (AUT)

■ 25 Photograph from a folder for the department store
Breuninger, here presenting designer fashions. (GER)

■ 22-24 Beispiele der Aufnahmen aus einem Katalog mit
dem Titel «Classic Loden Collection» von *Salko,* Salzburg.
Als Kulisse diente Schloss Fuschl, das Mitte des 15. Jahrhunderts von Erzbischof Friedrich IV Truchsass von Emmerberg
als Feudalunterkunft für seine Jagdgäste gebaut wurde und
heute ein Luxushotel ist. (AUT)

■ 25 Aufnahme aus einem Prospekt des Textilhauses Breuninger, das hier Designer-Mode vorstellt. (GER)

■ 22-24 Exemples des photos illustrant un catalogue de
lodens, «Classic Loden Collection», de *Salko* à Salzbourg. Le
décor est constitué par le château de Fuschl que l'archévê-
que Frédéric IV Truchsass d'Emmerberg érigea au milieu du
XVe siècle pour ses compagnons de chasse, et qui a été
transformé de nos jours en hôtel de luxe. (AUT)

■ 25 Photo pour un dépliant des grands magasins Breuninger: modèles de qualité design. (GER)

PHOTOGRAPHER:
Cheryl Koralik
CLIENT:
Mimmina
ART DIRECTOR:
Nando Miglio
AGENCY:
Modenese & Modenese
■ 26–29

■ 26-29 Examples of the polychrome printed chamois photographs from a catalog for fashions by *Mimmina*. The catalog is comprised exclusively of photographs, the trademark, and the address of the producer. A matte, yellowish-toned paper was used. (ITA)

■ 26-29 Beispiele der mehrfarbig gedruckten Chamois-Aufnahmen aus einem Katalog für Mode von *Mimmina*. Der Katalog besteht ausschliesslich aus den Photos, dem Markenzeichen und der Adresse des Herstellers. Es wurde ein mattes, gelblich getöntes Papier verwendet. (ITA)

■ 26-29 Photos chamois reproduites en polychromie dans un catalogue de modes *Mimmina*. Aucune de ces illustrations n'est légendée. A part les photos, le catalogue ne comprend que la marque déposée et l'adresse du fabricant. Il est imprimé sur un papier mat légèrement teinté en jaune. (ITA)

PHOTOGRAPHER:
TAMOTSU FUJII
CLIENT:
PASHU CO., LTD.
ART DIRECTOR:
HIROSHI TAKAHARA
DESIGNER:
HIROSHI TAKAHARA/
MAYUMI OKA
AGENCY:
HIROSHI TAKAHARA
DESIGN OFFICE
◄■ 30-33

PHOTOGRAPHER:
DOUGLAS KEEVE
PUBLISHER:
ZOOM
ART DIRECTOR:
JOËL LAROCHE
■ 34

■ 30-33 Typical black-and-white photographs from a catalog on men's fashion for spring and summer 1987, issued by the Japanese manufacturer *Shin Hosokawa.* (JPN)

■ 34 From a feature in *Zoom,* in which *Polaroid* photographs by various photographers are shown. This is a fashion photograph by Douglas Keeve. (FRA)

■ 30-33 Schwarzweissaufnahmen aus einem Katalog über Herrenmode für Frühjahr und Sommer 1987, herausgegeben von dem japanischen Hersteller *Shin Hosokawa.* (JPN)

■ 34 Aus einem Beitrag in *Zoom,* in dem *Polaroid*-Aufnahmen verschiedener Photographen vorgestellt werden. Hier eine Modeaufnahme von Douglas Keeve. (FRA)

■ 30-33 Exemples des photos noir et blanc qui illustrent le catalogue printemps/été 1987 des modes masculines du fabricant japonais *Shin Hosokawa.* (JPN)

■ 34 Photo pleine page tirée d'un article de *Zoom* où divers photographes présentent leurs travaux en *Polaroïd.* On voit ici une photo de mode de Douglas Keeve. (FRA)

PHOTOGRAPHER:
DEBORAH TURBEVILLE
CLIENT:
EMANUEL UNGARO
ART DIRECTOR:
ALBERTO NODOLINI
AGENCY:
STUDIO FILOMENO
■ 35, 36

■ 35, 36 From a campaign with double-spread photographs for *Emanuel Ungaro,* which appeared in the French as well as in the Italian edition of *Vogue.*

■ 35, 36 Aus einer Kampagne mit doppelseitigen Aufnahmen für *Emanuel Ungaro,* die sowohl in der französischen als auch in der italienischen Ausgabe von *Vogue* erschien.

■ 35, 36 Exemples d'une campagne *Emanuel Ungaro* illustrée de photos double page, reproduites aussi bien dans l'édition française que dans l'édition italienne de *Vogue.*

PHOTOGRAPHER:
Barry Lategan
CLIENT:
Deutsche VOGUE
PUBLISHER:
Condé Nast Verlag GmbH
ART DIRECTOR:
Angelica Blechschmidt
■ 38-42

■ 38-42 "Excursion in blue and white" is the title of this fashion feature in the German edition of *Vogue* to which these photographs belong. These two colors express the mood of beach, wind, water, and summer skies. (GER)

■ 38-42 «Streifzug in Blau-Weiss» ist der Titel dieses Modebeitrags in der deutschen Ausgabe von *Vogue*. Die mit diesen Farben verbundenen Gedanken an Strand, Wind, Wasser und Sommerhimmel kommen hier zum Ausdruck. (GER)

■ 38-42 «Balade en bleu et blanc» - c'est sous ce titre qu'a paru l'article de mode illustré de ces photos dans l'édition allemande de *Vogue*. Les couleurs sont associées à des images de plage, de vent, d'eau et de ciel d'été. (GER)

PHOTOGRAPHER:
ALBERT WATSON
CLIENT:
BLUMARINE
ART DIRECTOR:
MANUELA PAVESI
AGENCY:
PRIMO PUNTO SRL.
■ 43–48

■ 43–48 Cover shot and further photographs from a catalog for fashion by *Blumarine* which was inserted as a supplement to a special issue of *Vogue Italia*. Photographs only were shown – without any comment or addition. (ITA)

■ 43–48 Umschlagphoto und weitere Aufnahmen aus einem Katalog für Mode von *Blumarine*, der einer Sonderausgabe von *Vogue Italia* beigefügt war. Es werden ausschliesslich Aufnahmen gezeigt, ohne jeglichen Zusatz. (ITA)

■ 43–48 Illustration de couverture et photos intérieures d'un catalogue des modes *Blumarine* encarté dans un numéro spécial de *Vogue Italia*. Aucune de ces photos n'est légendée, ce qui en augmente l'impact. (ITA)

PHOTOGRAPHER:
John Curtis
CLIENT:
Kate Joyce Designs
ART DIRECTOR:
Dean Noble/John Curtis
DESIGNER:
Dean Noble
AGENCY:
Wildman Advertising
■ 49, 50

■ 49, 50 Double-spread photograph from inside a black-and-white printed catalog, and also the catalog's cover shot, promoting spring fashion by *Kate Joyce*. (USA)

■ 51 Fashion photograph used as self-promotion for photographer Hans Neleman. (USA)

■ 49, 50 Doppelseitige Aufnahme aus dem Inhalt und Umschlagphoto für einen in Schwarzweiss gedruckten Katalog für Frühjahrsmode von *Kate Joyce*. (USA)

■ 51 Als Eigenwerbung des Photographen Hans Neleman verwendete Modeaufnahme. (USA)

■ 49, 50 Photo intérieure double page et photo de couverture d'un catalogue noir et blanc servant à la présentation des modes printanières de *Kate Joyce*. (USA)

■ 51 Photo de mode que le photographe Hans Neleman utilise à des fins autopromotionnelles. (USA)

PHOTOGRAPHER:
HANS NELEMAN
CLIENT:
HANS NELEMAN STUDIO
ART DIRECTOR:
MYLENE TUREK
■ 51

PHOTOGRAPHER:
BARRY LATEGAN
■ 52

PHOTOGRAPHER:
SHEILA METZNER
■ 53

■ 52-54 Photographs appearing in *Vogue Italia*, from an ad campaign for fabrics from Prato, a town to the north of Florence. In connection with a trade fair, internationally famous photographers were commissioned to freely interpret this center of Italy's wool and fabric industry. (ITA)

■ 52-54 Aufnahmen aus einer in *Vogue Italia* erschienenen Werbekampagne für Stoffe aus Prato, einer Stadt in der Nähe von Florenz. Verschiedene, international bekannte Photographen erhielten den Auftrag, diesen Industriezweig durch eine freie Interpretation darzustellen. (ITA)

■ 52-54 Photos illustrant une campagne publicitaire dans *Vogue Italia* en faveur des textiles de la ville de Prato près de Florence. A l'occasion d'une foire d'échantillons divers photographes de réputation internationale ont été chargés d'interpréter librement cette branche de l'industrie. (ITA)

CLIENT:
PRATO EXPO/CASSA DI RISPARMI E DEPOSITI DI PRATO
ART DIRECTOR:
ALBERTO NODOLINI

PHOTOGRAPHER:
ART KANE
■ 54

AGENCY:
FLOR/ITALIA
■ 52-54

PHOTOGRAPHER:
BILL SILANO
■ 55

PHOTOGRAPHER:
HORST
■ 56

PHOTOGRAPHER:
DEBORAH TURBEVILLE
■ 57

PHOTOGRAPHER:
ROBERT MAPPLETHORPE
■ 58

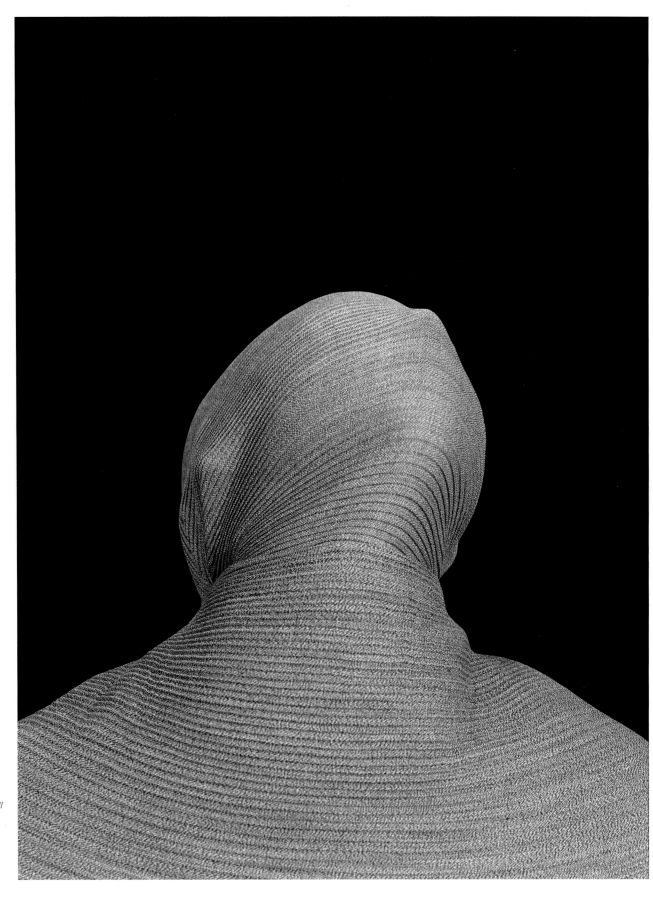

CLIENT:
*PRATO EXPO/CASSA DI RISPARMI
E DEPOSITI DI PRATO*
ART DIRECTOR:
ALBERTO NODOLINI
AGENCY:
FLOR/ITALIA
■ 55-58

■ 55-58 Further examples of the 20 full-page photos by various renowned photographers, from an ad campaign to promote fabrics from Prato, near Florence, on the occasion of a trade fair. (ITA)

■ 55-58 Weitere Beispiele der insgesamt 20 ganzseitigen Aufnahmen von verschiedenen berühmten Photographen, aus einer Werbekampagne für Stoffe aus Prato bei Florenz anlässlich einer Messe. (ITA)

■ 55-58 Exemples des 20 illustrations pleine page réalisées par divers photographes de renom pour une campagne vantant les mérites des textiles de Prato à l'occasion d'une foire. (ITA)

PHOTOGRAPHER:
Albert Watson
CLIENT:
Blumarine
ART DIRECTOR:
Manuela Pavesi
AGENCY:
Primo Punto Srl
■ 60

■ 60 Photograph from an advertisement for a creation by fashion designer Anna Molinari for *Blumarine*. (ITA)

■ 61 Double-spread photograph with Western-style fashion, from a feature in the French *Vogue*. Location for the shot was St. Moritz in Switzerland. (FRA)

■ 60 Aufnahme aus einem Inserat für ein Modell der Modeschöpferin Anna Molinari für *Blumarine*. (ITA)

■ 61 Doppelseitige Aufnahme mit Mode im Western-Stil, aus einem Beitrag in der französischen *Vogue*. Das Photo wurde in St. Moritz, Schweiz, gemacht. (FRA)

■ 60 Photo illustrant une annonce pour un modèle *Blumarine* de la créatrice de mode Anna Molinari. (ITA)

■ 61 Photo double page de modes de style western, dans un article de l'édition française de *Vogue*. Cette photo a été réalisée à Saint-Moritz, en Suisse. (FRA)

PHOTOGRAPHER:
HANS FEURER
CLIENT:
VOGUE PARIS
PUBLISHER:
CONDÉ NAST SA
ART DIRECTOR:
PAUL WAGNER
■ 61

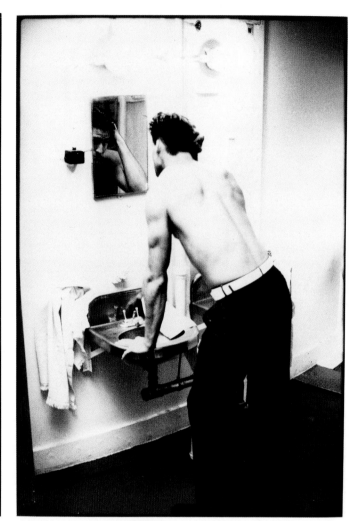

PHOTOGRAPHER:
CLAUS WICKRATH
CLIENT:
L'UOMO
PUBLISHER:
CONDÉ NAST S. P.A.
ART DIRECTOR:
ARMANDO CHITOLINA
■ 62-66

■ 62-66 On board the American warship "U.S.S. Alabama". Photos from a fashion feature entitled "Navy Look" appearing in the Italian men's fashion magazine *L'Uomo*. (ITA)

■ 62-66 An Bord des amerikanischen Kriegsschiffes «U.S.S. Alabama» gemachte Modeaufnahmen, aus einem Beitrag unter dem Titel «Navy Look» im Herrenmodemagazin *L'Uomo*. (ITA)

■ 62-66 Photos réalisées à bord du bâtiment de guerre américain «U.S.S. Alabama», pour un article intitulé «Navy Look», paru dans le magazine de modes masculines *L'Uomo*. (ITA)

■ 67, 68 Photographs from a feature on ready-to-wear fashions from Paris, appearing in *Jardin des Modes.* (SWI)

■ 69, 70 Anatomy as art form. American photographer Bruce Weber created a new style of fashion photography with his shots for designer Calvin Klein. (USA)

■ 67, 68 Aufnahmen aus einem Beitrag über Prêt-à-porter-Mode aus Paris, erschienen in *Jardin des Modes.* (SWI)

■ 69, 70 Anatomie als Kunstform. Der Amerikaner Bruce Weber schuf eine neue Mode-Photographie mit seinen Aufnahmen für den Textil-Designer Calvin Klein. (USA)

■ 67, 68 Photos pleine page illustrant un article sur le prêt-à-porter parisien publié dans le *Jardin des Modes.* (SWI)

■ 69, 70 L'anatomie promue forme d'art. L'Américain Bruce Weber initie un nouveau style de photographie de mode dans la série réalisée pour le designer Calvin Klein. (GER)

PHOTOGRAPHER:
ALEXANDRO ESTERI
PUBLISHER:
JARDIN DES MODES
ART DIRECTOR:
ALAIN CASTORIANO
■ 67, 68

PHOTOGRAPHER:
Bruce Weber
CLIENT:
Calvin Klein
Industries, Inc.
ART DIRECTOR:
Sam Shahid
AGENCY:
CRK Advertising
■ 69, 70

PHOTOGRAPHER:
STEVE HIETT
PUBLISHER:
MARIE CLAIRE
ART DIRECTOR:
WALTER ROSPERT
■ 71

■ 71 Double-spread photograph from a feature in *Marie Claire* on the 150th anniversary of the *Hermès* fashion house. All the photographs for the article were taken on location in Deauville, the French resort. (FRA)

■ 72-75 Examples of the full-page chamois photographs from a catalog of fashions by *Nicole*, for spring and summer 1987. *75* was used for the title page. (JPN)

■ 71 Doppelseitige Aufnahme aus einem Beitrag in *Marie Claire* zum hundertfünfzigsten Geburtstag des Modehauses *Hermès*. Alle Photos für den Artikel wurden im Sommer 1987 in Deauville gemacht. (FRA)

■ 72-75 Beispiele der ganzseitigen Chamois-Aufnahmen aus einem Katalog für Mode der Marke *Nicole*, Frühjahr und Sommer 1987. *75* wurde für die Titelseite verwendet. (JPN)

■ 71 Photo double page pour un article du *Marie Claire* consacré au 150e anniversaire du grand couturier *Hermès*. Toutes les photos figurant dans cet article ont été prises à Deauville durant l'été 1987. (FRA)

■ 72-75 Exemples des photos chamois pleine page illustrant le catalogue printemps/été 1987 des modes *Nicole*. La fig. *75* a été utilisée pour la couverture. (JPN)

PHOTOGRAPHER:
Javier Vollhonrat
CLIENT:
Nicole Co., Ltd.
ART DIRECTOR:
Hiroshi Takahara
DESIGNER:
Hiroshi Takahara
AGENCY:
Hiroshi Takahara
Design Office
■ 72-75

PHOTOGRAPHER:
Sante D'Orazio
CLIENT:
Deutsche VOGUE
PUBLISHER:
Condé Nast Verlag GmbH
ART DIRECTOR:
Angelica Blechschmidt
■ 76

PHOTOGRAPHER:
BARRY LATEGAN
CLIENT:
VOGUE ITALIA
PUBLISHER:
CONDÉ NAST S.P.A.
ART DIRECTOR:
ALBERTO NODOLINI
■ 77, 78

■ 76 Photograph on the introductory double spread to an article in the German *Vogue* about a new restrained fashion from Italy, distinctive for its simple cut and luxurious materials. (GER)

■ 77, 78 "Romantic variations on a strict fashion" – photos in black and white from a fashion feature on this subject in *Vogue Italia*. (ITA)

■ 76 Aufnahme der einleitenden Doppelseite zu einem Artikel in der deutschen *Vogue* über eine neue, stille Mode aus Italien, die sich durch schlichte Schnitte und luxuriöse Stoffe auszeichnet. (GER)

■ 77, 78 «Romantische Abweichungen einer strengen Mode», Aufnahmen in Schwarzweiss aus einem Modebeitrag in *Vogue Italia*. (ITA)

■ 76 Photo double page en tête d'un article que l'édition allemande de *Vogue* consacre à une nouvelle mode calme venue d'Italie, caractérisée par une coupe sobre et l'emploi de tissus proprement somptueux. (GER)

■ 77, 78 «Incartades romantiques d'une mode autrement sévère»: photos noir et blanc pour un article de *Vogue Italia*. (ITA)

PHOTOGRAPHER:
Patrick Demarchelier
PUBLISHER:
Marie Claire
ART DIRECTOR:
Walter Rospert
■ 79

PHOTOGRAPHER:
PAOLO ROVERSI
CLIENT:
ROMEO GIGLI
■ 80

PHOTOGRAPHER:
DAVID BAILEY
CLIENT:
GIANNI VERSACE
ART DIRECTOR:
PAUL BECK/
DONATELLA VERSACE
■ 81

■ 79 From an article in *Marie Claire* about the new one-piece swimsuits for summer 1987. (FRA)

■ 80 Photograph from a double-spread ad for fashions created by *Romeo Gigli*, published in *Vogue Italia*. (ITA)

■ 81 From a full-page ad promoting fashions designed by *Gianni Versace* in the French *Vogue*. (FRA)

■ 79 Aus einem Beitrag in *Marie Claire* über die neuen einteiligen Badeanzüge für den Sommer 1987. (FRA)

■ 80 Aufnahme aus einer doppelseitigen Anzeige für Mode von *Romeo Gigli*, erschienen in *Vogue Italia*. (ITA)

■ 81 Aus einem ganzseitigen Inserat für Mode von *Gianni Versace* in der französischen *Vogue*. (FRA)

■ 79 Pour un article de *Marie Claire* consacré aux nouveaux maillots de bain une pièce de l'été 1987. (FRA)

■ 80 Photo illustrant une annonce double page pour les modes *Romeo Gigli* parue dans *Vogue Italia*. (ITA)

■ 81 Pour une annonce pleine page des créations *Gianni Versace* dans l'édition française de *Vogue*. (FRA)

PHOTOGRAPHER:
BILL SUMNER
CLIENT:
BILL SUMNER PHOTOGRAPHY
ART DIRECTOR:
PETER MOORE/NIKE DESIGN
■ 82

■ 82 Fashion photograph used as self-promotion for photographer Bill Sumner. (USA)

■ 83 Double-spread photo from an advertisement for *Nike* sports shoes – nothing added to the photo apart from the trademark. (USA)

■ 82 Als Eigenwerbung des Photographen Bill Sumner verwendete Modeaufnahme. (USA)

■ 83 Doppelseitige Aufnahme aus einem Inserat für *Nike*-Sportschuhe, das nur aus dem Photo und dem Schriftzug besteht. (USA)

■ 82 Photo de mode que le photographe Bill Sumner utilise à des fins autopromotionnelles. (USA)

■ 83 Photo double page, sans légende, avec la griffe *Nike*, pour une annonce publicitaire de ce fabricant de chaussures de sport. (USA)

PHOTOGRAPHER:
STEPHEN WILKES
CLIENT:
STEPHEN WILKES
PHOTOGRAPHY, INC./
NIKE, INC.
ART DIRECTOR:
STEVE SANDSTROM
AGENCY:
WIEDEN & KENNEDY
■ 83

PHOTOGRAPHER:
CHIMÈNE LASSERRE
CLIENT:
HOM INTERNATIONAL
ART DIRECTOR:
GÉRARD DRIANCOURT
AGENCY:
PUBLICIS MÉDITERRANÉE
◄■ 84

PHOTOGRAPHER:
HANS FEURER
CLIENT:
VOGUE PARIS
PUBLISHER:
CONDÉ NAST SA
ART DIRECTOR:
PAUL WAGNER
■ 85, 86

■ 84 Black-and-white photograph from an advertisement to promote the swimwear fashion collection by *Hom.* (ITA)

■ 85, 86 Photographs from an article in the French *Vogue,* concerning fitness training, and its related clothing and body care. (FRA)

■ 84 Schwarzweissaufnahme aus einem Inserat für die Bademodekollektion von *Hom.* (ITA)

■ 85, 86 Aufnahmen aus einem Artikel in der französischen *Vogue,* der sich mit Fitness-Training, der passenden Kleidung und Körperpflege befasst. (FRA)

■ 84 Photo noir et blanc figurant dans une annonce des collections de modes de plage *Hom.* (ITA)

■ 85, 86 Photos illustrant un article que l'édition française de *Vogue* consacre à la culture physique, aux trainings et vêtements de sport et aux soins du corps. (FRA)

PHOTOGRAPHER:
CLAUS WICKRATH
CLIENT:
L'UOMO
PUBLISHER:
CONDÉ NAST S.P.A.
ART DIRECTOR:
ARMANDO CHITOLINA
■ 87-90

■ 87-91 Examples of the photographs from an article in the men's fashion magazine *L'Uomo,* in which clothing items for various sports and their officials are presented. (ITA)

■ 87-91 Aufnahmen aus einem Artikel im Herrenmodemagazin *L'Uomo,* in dem Kleidung für verschiedene Sportarten und für Funktionäre vorgestellt wird. (ITA)

■ 87-91 Photos illustrant un article du magazine de modes masculines *L'Uomo:* vêtements de sports pour différentes disciplines, vêtements pour entraîneurs et officiels. (ITA)

PHOTOGRAPHER:
FLAVIO BONETTI
CLIENT:
L'UOMO
PUBLISHER:
CONDÉ NAST S.P.A.
ART DIRECTOR:
ARMANDO CHITOLINA
■ 91

PHOTOGRAPHER:
LANCE STAEDLER
CLIENT:
L'UOMO
PUBLISHER:
CONDÉ NAST S.P.A.
ART DIRECTOR:
ARMANDO CHITOLINA
■ 92, 93

■ 92, 93 Swimwear demonstrated by the stars of Italian acrobatic diving, from an article featuring this aquatic sport discipline and the Italian Olympic team, in *L'Uomo*. (ITA)

■ 92, 93 Bademode, von den Stars der italienischen Kunstspringer demonstriert, aus einem Artikel über diese Sportart und die italienische Olympiamannschaft in *L'Uomo*. (ITA)

■ 92, 93 Modes de plage présentées par des vedettes italiennes du plongeon de haut vol. Article dans *L'Uomo* sur cette discipline sportive et sur l'équipe olympique nationale. (ITA)

Photographer:
Manfred Vogelsänger
Client:
Manfred Vogelsänger
Art Director:
Manfred Vogelsänger
Designer:
Uwe Loesch
Studio:
Vogelsänger Studio GmbH
■ 94, 95

■ 94, 95 Photographs from a calendar by Manfred Vogel-sänger. Most of the shots were taken in the studios with room sets and photographic wallpaper. (GER)

■ 96 Fashion photograph used as self-promotion for photographer Joe Baraban. (USA)

■ 94, 95 Aufnahmen aus einem Kalender des Photographen Manfred Vogelsänger. Die meisten Bilder entstanden im Studio mit gezimmerten Kulissen und Phototapeten. (GER)

■ 96 Als Eigenwerbung des Photographen Joe Baraban verwendete Modeaufnahme. (USA)

■ 94, 95 Photos illustrant un calendrier du photographe Manfred Vogelsänger. La plupart de ces images ont été réalisées en studio (décors construits, coulisses photo). (GER)

■ 96 Photo de mode que le photographe Joe Baraban utilise à des fins autopromotionnelles (USA)

PHOTOGRAPHER:
JOE BARABAN
CLIENT:
JOE BARABAN
DESIGNER:
JOHN WEAVER
AGENCY:
GLUTH WEAVER
■ 96

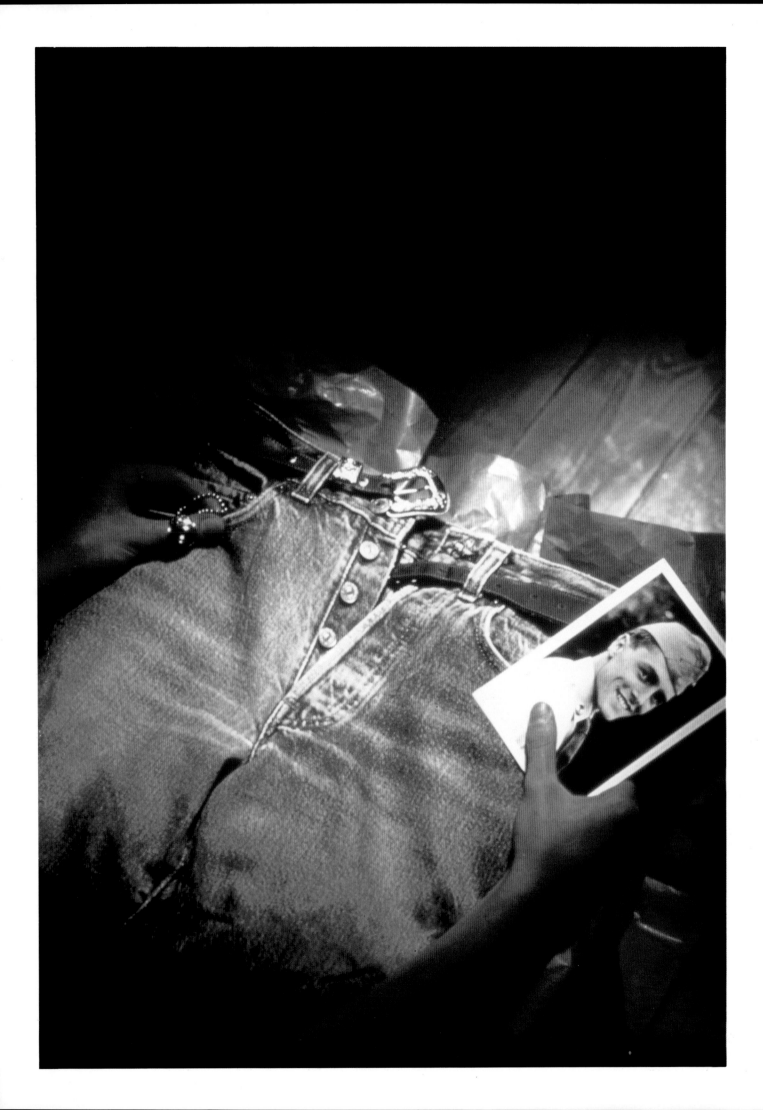

PHOTOGRAPHER:
DAVE MOASE
CLIENT:
LEVI STRAUSS & CO.
ART DIRECTOR:
DENNIS LEWIS/
GÜNTER BITTER
AGENCY:
BARTLE, BOGLE, HEGARTY/
McCANN-ERICKSON FRANKFURT
◀■ 97

PHOTOGRAPHER:
JACQUES SCHUMACHER
CLIENT:
OPTYL HOLDING GMBH & CO.
ART DIRECTOR:
NORBERT HEROLD
DESIGNER:
RALPH TAUBENBERGER
AGENCY:
HEYE + PARTNER
■ 98, 99

■ 97 Full-page photograph from an advertisement for *Levi's* jeans. (GER)

■ 98, 99 Photographs for the July and May sheets of a calendar for *Vienna Lines* eyeglasses. (GER)

■ 97 Ganzseitige Aufnahme aus einem Inserat für *Levi's*-Jeans. (GER)

■ 98, 99 Aufnahmen für die Juli- und Mai-Blätter eines Wandkalenders mit Brillen der Marke *Vienna Lines*. (GER)

■ 97 Photo pleine page illustrant une annonce en faveur des jeans *Levi's*. (GER)

■ 98, 99 Photos ornant les feuillets de juillet et de mai d'un calendrier mural de la lunetterie *Vienna Lines*. (GER)

Photographer:
Jean Larivière
Client:
Vogue Paris
Publisher:
Condé Nast SA
Art Director:
Paul Wagner
■ 100–102

■ 100–102 Double-spread photographs from an editorial feature in the French *Vogue* about *Louis Vuitton,* luggage producer, entitled "Imaginary Journey". Jean Larivière took the photographs in the old factory at Asnières with neither flash nor montage. (FRA)

■ 100–102 Doppelseitige Aufnahmen aus einem redaktionellen Beitrag in der französischen *Vogue* unter dem Titel «Imaginäre Reise» über *Louis Vuitton,* Hersteller von Reisegepäck. Jean Larivière machte diese Photos in der alten Fabrik in Asnières ohne Blitzlicht und Montage. (FRA)

■ 100–102 Photos double page illustrant un article de l'édition française de *Vogue* qui évoque l'épopée du maroquinier *Louis Vuitton* sous le titre de «Voyage imaginaire». Jean Larivière a réalisé ces images dans la vieille usine d'Asnières sans utiliser de flash ni aucun artifice de montage. (FRA)

PHOTOGRAPHER:
Dieter Henneka
CLIENT:
MCM-Reisegepäck
ART DIRECTOR:
Urs Schwerzmann
DESIGNER:
Urs Schwerzmann
AGENCY:
Büro Schwerzmann
■ 107–112

■ 107-112 Photographs from an ad campaign for handmade suitcases and bags by MCM. Locations are always given (from l. to r.): Hotel Danieli, Venice; Hotel des Borromees, Stresa; Villa Cipriani, Asolo; Hotel des Iles Borromees, Stresa; Park Hotel, Sienna. (GER)

■ 107-112 Aus einer Werbekampagne für Koffer und Taschen der Marke MCM, die in Handarbeit hergestellt werden. Die Aufnahmeorte v.l.n.r.: Hotel Danieli, Venedig; Hotel des Iles Borromees, Stresa; Villa Cipriani, Asolo; Hotel des Iles Borromees, Stresa; Park-Hotel, Siena. (GER)

■ 107-112 Photos utilisées dans une campagne pour les valises et sacs MCM de fabrication artisanale. Le site est indiqué à chaque fois: de g. à dr., Hôtel Danieli, Venise; Hôtel des Îles Borromées, Stresa; Villa Cipriani, Asolo; Hôtel des Îles Borromées, Stresa; Park-Hôtel, Sienne. (GER)

PHOTOGRAPHER:
CHERYL KLAUSS
■ 113–115

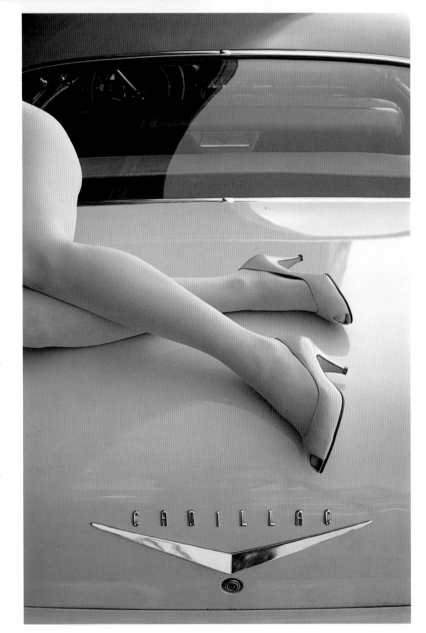

■ 113–115 Unpublished photographs for shoe promotion, devoted to the theme of color. (USA)

■ 116 Full-page photograph from an advertisement for shoes marketed under the *Italo Colombo* label. (ITA)

■ 117 From a double-spread magazine advertisement for *Casadei* shoes. (ITA)

■ 113–115 Unveröffentlichte Aufnahmen für Schuhwerbung, ganz auf das Thema Farbe ausgerichtet. (USA)

■ 116 Ganzseitige Aufnahme aus einem Inserat für Schuhe der Marke *Italo Colombo*. (ITA)

■ 117 Aus einem doppelseitigen Zeitschrifteninserat für *Casadei*-Schuhe. (ITA)

■ 113–115 Photos inédites pour une publicité de chaussures entièrement axée sur les coloris. (USA)

■ 116 Photo pleine page pour une annonce du chasseur italien *Italo Colombo*. (ITA)

■ 117 Pour une annonce de magazine double page servant à la publicité des chaussures *Casadei*. (ITA)

PHOTOGRAPHER:
ORIGONE E ORIANI
CLIENT:
ITALO COLOMBO
ART DIRECTOR:
RAFFAELE ORIGONE/
MATTEO ORIANI
STUDIO:
GRAZIA GAY
■ 116

PHOTOGRAPHER:
PIERO GEMELLI
CLIENT:
CASADEI S.P.A.
ART DIRECTOR:
BARBARA FALANGA
STUDIO:
BARBARA FALANGA
■ 117

PHOTOGRAPHER:
Tsuyoshi Fuseya
CLIENT:
Antas Co., Ltd.
ART DIRECTOR:
Matsuhiro Kobayashi
DESIGNER:
Matsuhiro Kobayashi
■ 118

■ 118 Full-page photograph for shoes by *Stéphane Kélian,* of Paris. (JPN)

■ 118 Ganzseitige Aufnahme für Schuhe der Marke *Stéphane Kélian,* Paris. (JPN)

■ 118 Photo pleine page pour les créations de chaussures *Stéphane Kélian,* Paris. (JPN)

COSMETICS

COSMÉTIQUES

KOSMETIK

COSMÉTIQUES

PHOTOGRAPHER:
PIERO GEMELLI
CLIENT:
VOGUE ITALIA
PUBLISHER:
CONDÉ NAST S.P.A.
ART DIRECTOR:
ALBERTO NODOLINI
◀■ 119

PHOTOGRAPHER:
BARRY LATEGAN
CLIENT:
DEUTSCHE VOGUE
PUBLISHER:
CONDÉ NAST VERLAG GMBH
ART DIRECTOR:
ANGELICA BLECHSCHMIDT
■ 120

■ 119 "Fashion in the Bottle" is the title of the feature in *Vogue Italia* to which this photograph belongs. The new perfume "Basile" is presented. (ITA)

■ 120 Photograph for the introductory double spread to an article in the German *Vogue* about beauty care and fitness in summer. (GER)

■ 119 «Mode in der Flasche» ist der Titel des Beitrags in *Vogue Italia*, zu dem diese Aufnahme gehört. Hier wird das neue Parfum «Basile» vorgestellt. (ITA)

■ 120 Aufnahme für die einleitende Doppelseite zu einem Beitrag in der deutschen *Vogue* über Schönheitspflege und Fitness im Sommer. (GER)

■ 119 «La mode en flacon» – c'est sous ce titre qu'a paru l'article de *Vogue Italia* où figure cette photo, qui présente le nouveau parfum «Basile». (ITA)

■ 120 Photo illustrant la double page initiale d'un article de l'édition allemande de *Vogue* où il est question de soins de beauté et de mise en condition physique en été. (GER)

■ 121 Personal study of a perfume flacon which Milanese photographer Alberto Longari uses for self-promotional purposes. (ITA)

■ 122 As self promotion, a photograph of a perfume bottle taken by Jim McCrary of Los Angeles. (USA)

■ 121 Persönliche Studie einer Parfumflasche, die der Mailänder Photograph Alberto Longari als Eigenwerbung verwendet. (ITA)

■ 122 Als Eigenwerbung verwendete Aufnahme einer Parfumflasche von Jim McCrary, Los Angeles. (USA)

■ 121 Etude personnelle d'un flacon de parfum. Le photographe milanais Alberto Longari, qui l'a réalisée, l'utilise pour sa promotion. (ITA)

■ 122 Photo d'un flacon de parfum, par Jim McCrary de Los Angeles. Elle lui sert pour son autopromotion. (USA)

PHOTOGRAPHER:
ALBERTO LONGARI
CLIENT:
ALBERTO LONGARI
ART DIRECTOR:
ALBERTO LONGARI
■ 121

PHOTOGRAPHER:
JIM MCCRARY
CLIENT:
JIM MCCRARY
ART DIRECTOR:
JIM MCCRARY
►■ 122

PHOTOGRAPHER:
PIERO GEMELLI
CLIENT:
VOGUE ITALIA
PUBLISHER:
CONDÉ NAST S.P.A.
ART DIRECTOR:
ALBERTO NODOLINI
■ 123, 124

■ 123, 124 Full-page photo-graph from a feature in *Vogue Italia* on cosmetics. Shown is a night cream by *Orlane* and a lipstick by *Paloma Picasso*. (ITA)

■ 123, 124 Ganzseitige Auf-nahmen aus einem Beitrag in *Vogue Italia* über Kosme-tik: eine Nachtcrème von *Orlane* und ein Lippenstift von *Paloma Picasso*. (ITA)

■ 123, 124 Photos pleine page illustrant un article de cosmétique de *Vogue Italia:* une crème de nuit d'*Orlane,* un rouge à lèvres de *Paloma Picasso*. (ITA)

■ 125, 126 Full-page portrait photographs in black and white of Karl Lagerfeld and Paloma Picasso, and color shots of their perfume flacons, from a special campaign in *Vogue Paris*. (FRA)

■ 127 *Shiseido* - color accents by Serge Lutens"; photograph from a double-spread ad for *Shiseido*'s eyeshadow palette for spring/summer 1987. (JPN)

■ 125, 126 Ganzseitige Porträtaufnahmen in Schwarzweiss von Karl Lagerfeld und Paloma Picasso und Farbphotos der von ihnen kreierten Parfumflaschen aus einer Kampagne in *Vogue Paris*. (FRA)

■ 127 *Shiseido* - in Farbakzenten von Serge Lutens»; Aufnahme aus einer doppelseitigen Anzeige für die Lidschatten-Palette Frühjahr/Sommer 1987 von *Shiseido*. (JPN)

■ 125, 126 Portraits pleine page, en noir et blanc, de Karl Lagerfeld et de Paloma Picasso et photos couleurs des flacons de parfum portant leur nom. D'un campagne spécial dans *Vogue Paris*. (FRA)

■ 127 «*Shiseido* - accents chromatiques de Serge Lutens»: photo illustrant une annonce double page pour la gamme des ombres à paupières *Shiseido*, printemps/été 1987. (JPN)

PHOTOGRAPHER:
Jeanloup Sieff
Alain P. Méry (Perfume)
CLIENT:
Promotion VOGUE Paris
PUBLISHER:
Condé Nast SA
ART DIRECTOR:
Paul Wagner
◄■ 125, 126

PHOTOGRAPHER:
Serge Lutens
CLIENT:
Shiseido Co., Ltd.
ART DIRECTOR:
Serge Lutens/Isamu Hanauchi
AGENCY:
Shiseido Co., Ltd.
►■ 127

PHOTOGRAPHER:
PIERO GEMELLI
CLIENT:
VOGUE ITALIA
PUBLISHER:
CONDÉ NAST S.P.A.
ART DIRECTOR:
ALBERTO NODOLINI
■ 128-130

■ 128-130 "Color as focal point of the new makeup generation." Full-page photographs from a feature in *Vogue Italia* in which the new colors for decorative cosmetics are presented. Shown is a rouge by *Chanel,* nailpolish by *Estée Lauder,* and a base teint by *Prescriptives.* (ITA)

■ 128-130 «Farbe im Mittelpunkt der neuen Make-Up-Kreationen.» Ganzseitige Aufnahmen aus einem Beitrag in *Vogue Italia,* in dem die neuen Farben für dekorative Kosmetik vorgestellt werden: ein Rouge von *Chanel,* Nagellack von *Estée Lauder* und ein Fond de Teint von *Prescriptives.* (ITA)

■ 128-130 «La couleur au centre des nouvelles créations de maquillages.» Photos pleine page illustrant un article de *Vogue Italia* où sont présentés les nouveaux coloris utilisés pour la cosmétique décorative: un rouge de *Chanel,* un vernis à ongles *Estée Lauder,* un fond de teint *Prescriptives.* (ITA)

PHOTOGRAPHER:
SHEILA METZNER
CLIENT:
FENDI PROFUMI S.P.A.
■ 131

■ 131 "La passione di Roma" (Roman Passion) is the name of the *Fendi* perfume which this full-page photograph is advertising. (ITA)

■ 131 «La passione di Roma» (römische Leidenschaft) ist der Name des Parfums von *Fendi*, für das mit dieser ganzseitigen Aufnahme geworben wird. (ITA)

■ 131 «La passione di Roma» (Passion romaine) – c'est le nom du nouveau parfum de *Fendi* présenté sur cette illustration photographique pleine page. (ITA)

OUTDOOR

EXTÉRIEURS

AUSSENAUFNAHMEN

EXTÉRIEURS

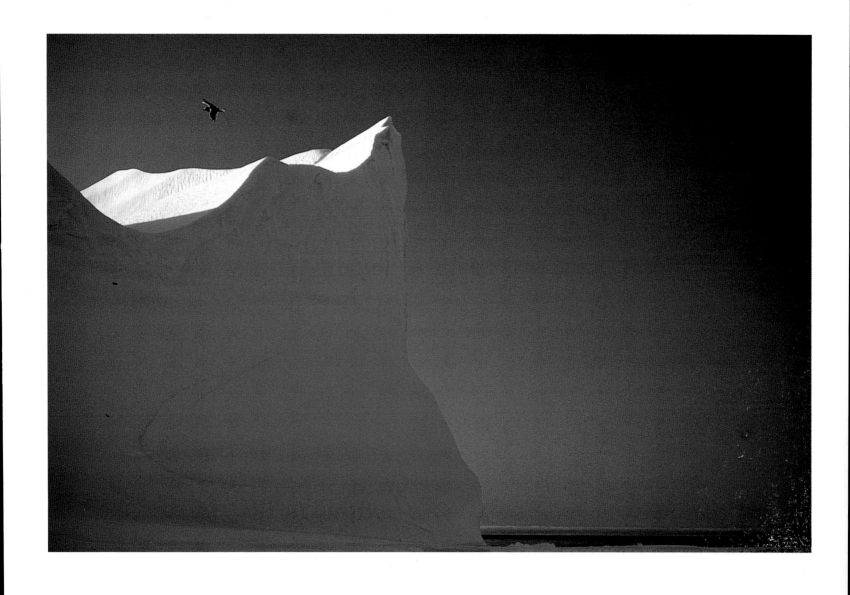

■ 132-135 Landscape photographs taken by Bruno J. Zehnder in the ice of the Antarctic. The chief problem for photographers working in extremely low temperature is not due to technical difficulties – Zehnder uses two *Nikon* cameras with mechanically controlled shutters – but with one's own fingers that are often numb with cold. (SWI)

■ 132-135 Im Eis der Antarktis entstandene Landschaftsbilder des Photographen Bruno J. Zehnder. Das Hauptproblem beim Photographieren in extremer Kälte liegt nicht im technischen Bereich – Zehnder arbeitet mit zwei *Nikon*-Kameras mit mechanisch gesteuerten Verschlusszeiten – sondern es sind die eigenen Finger, die Mühe machen. (SWI)

■ 132-135 Paysages du photographe Bruno J. Zehnder réalisés dans les glaces de l'Antarctique. Le problème principal de la photographie par un froid intense ne concerne pas l'équipement – dans le cas d'espèce, deux appareils *Nikon* à mise au point automatique –, mais l'homme, dont les doigts engourdis ont peine à tenir l'appareil. (SWI)

PHOTOGRAPHER:
RUURD DANKLOFF
PUBLISHER:
FOCUS
ART DIRECTOR:
RUURD DANKLOFF
STUDIO:
R. DANKLOFF PHOTOGRAPHY
■ 136, 137

■ 136, 137 "Nostalgia in Pastel Shades" is the title of an article in the Dutch photo magazine *Focus* devoted to photographer Ruurd Dankloff. Shown are examples of the photographs taken at beach resorts on the French and Belgian coasts. (NLD)

■ 136, 137 «Nostalgie in Pastelltönen» ist der Titel eines Beitrags im holländischen Photomagazin *Focus*, der dem Photographen Ruurd Dankloff gewidmet ist. Hier zwei Beispiele der Aufnahmen, die in Badeorten an den französischen und belgischen Küsten entstanden. (NLD)

■ 136, 137 «Nostalgie aux tons pastel», tel est le titre évocateur de l'article consacré au photographe Ruurd Dankloff dans le magazine photo hollandais *Focus*. On a ici deux échantillons des photos réalisées dans diverses stations balnéaires de France et de Belgique. (NLD)

PHOTOGRAPHER:
SANDERS NICOLSON
CLIENT:
J. BARBOUR & SONS LTD.
ART DIRECTOR:
STEVE MORRIS
AGENCY:
MORRIS, NICOLSON
& CARTWRIGHT
■ 138

■ 138 Photograph used in advertisements and posters issued by J. Barbour & Sons Ltd. (GBR)

■ 139 From the portfolio "Shoot at Joe's" of Joe Baraban, a Texas-based photographer. (USA)

■ 138 Für Anzeigen und Plakate verwendete Aufnahme im Auftrag von J. Barbour & Sons Ltd. (GBR)

■ 139 Aufnahme aus dem Portfolio «Shoot at Joe's» des texanischen Photographen Joe Baraban. (USA)

■ 138 Photo utilisée dans des annonces et sur des affiches pour le compte de J. Barbour & Sons Ltd. (GBR)

■ 139 Photo tirée du portfolio «Shoot at Joe's» de Joe Baraban, un photographe travaillant au Texas. (USA)

Photographer:
Joe Baraban
Client:
Joe Baraban
Designer:
John Weaver
Agency:
Gluth/Weaver
■ 139

PHOTOGRAPHER:
JAY MAISEL
PUBLISHER:
UNITED TECHNOLOGIES
ART DIRECTOR:
GORDON BOWMAN
DESIGNER:
DEREK BIRDSALL
AGENCY:
UNITED TECHNOLOGIES
■ 140–143

■ 140–143 Photographs from the book *Light on America* (United Technologies Corporation) with photographs by Jay Maisel. The photo titles are, from l. to r.: "Snowy Road, Jackson Hole, Wyoming"; "Coney Island Aerial, Brooklyn, New York"; "First Snow, Elizabeth Street, New York City"; and "Snow and Fences, Colorado". (USA)

■ 144 "Airdrie, Canada, 21:45 h" – Shot by Swiss photographer Christian Vogt. From a calendar published by the *Schweizer Baudokumentation* and used for adverdising purposes. (SWI)

■ 140–143 Aufnahmen aus dem Buch *Light on America* (United Technologies Corporation) mit Aufnahmen von Jay Maisel. Die Bildtitel v.l.n.r.: «Schneebedeckte Strasse, Jackson Hole, Wyoming»; «Coney Island aus der Luft, Brooklyn, N.Y.»; «Der erste Schnee, Elizabeth Street, New York City»; «Schnee und Zäune, Colorado». USA

■ 144 «Airdrie, Kanada, 21.45h» – Aufnahme des Schweizer Photographen Christian Vogt, die für einen Kalender verwendet wurde, den die *Schweizer Baudokumentation* für Werbezwecke drucken liess. (SWI)

■ 140–143 Photos tirées de l'ouvrage *Light on America* (United Technologies Corporation) illustré par Jay Maisel. De g. à dr.: «Route enneigée à Jackson Hole, dans le Wyoming»; «Vue aérienne de Coney Island, Brooklyn, dans l'Etat de New York»; «Première neige dans Elizabeth Street à New York»; «Neige et clôtures dans le Colorado». (USA)

■ 144 «Airdrie, Canada, 21 h 45» – œuvre du photographe suisse Christian Vogt reproduite dans un calendrier publié à des fins promotionnelles par la *Documentation suisse du bâtiment*. (SWI)

PHOTOGRAPHER:
Cristian Vogt
CLIENT:
Schweizer Baudokumentation
ART DIRECTOR:
Christian Vogt
AGENCY:
ZSM Zutter Sommer
Marketing AG
■ 144

PHOTOGRAPHER:
ARTHUR MEYERSON
CLIENT:
LARIMORE CREATIVE
ART DIRECTOR:
J.C. LARIMORE
DESIGNER:
J.C. LARIMORE
AGENCY:
LARIMORE CREATIVE
■ 145

PHOTOGRAPHER:
JIM MARSHALL
CLIENT:
JIM MARSHALL PHOTOGRAPHY
ART DIRECTOR:
DAVE MOORE
DESIGNER:
DAVE MOORE
AGENCY:
JIM MARSHALL PHOTOGRAPHY
■146

■145 "We can help you make an impact. In order for your message to be heard, it must first be seen." Self-promotional photograph for the marketing/design company Larimore Creative. (USA)

■146 Self-promotion for photographer Jim Marshall. (USA)

■145 «Wir können Ihnen helfen, Eindruck zu machen. Damit Ihre Botschaft gehört wird, muss sie zuerst gesehen werden.» Als Eigenwerbung der Marketing-Design-Firma Larimore Creative verwendete Aufnahme. (USA)

■146 Eigenwerbung des Photographen Jim Marshall. (USA)

■145 «Nous pouvons vous aider à frapper un coup décisif. Pour que votre message soit entendu, il doit d'abord être vu.» Photo autopromotionnelle de la société de marketing et de design Larimore Creative. (USA)

■146 Autopromotion du photographe Jim Marshall. (USA)

■147 Personal study by photographer Alan Geller: "Dunes in Death Valley". (USA)

■148, 149 "The ambivalence of blue" is the title of an article in HQ magazine, issued by the Heidelberger Printing Machine Co.. These shots from it were taken by German photographer Thomas Schmid. (GER)

■147 Persönliche Studie des Photographen Alan Geller: «Dünen im Death Valley (Tal des Todes)». (USA)

■148, 149 «Ambivalenzen des Blau» ist der Titel eines Artikels in dem von den Heidelberger Druckmaschinen herausgegebenen HQ-Magazin. Diese Aufnahmen von Thomas Schmid sind daraus entnommen. (GER)

■147 Etude personnelle due au photographe Alan Geller: «Dunes dans Death Valley (la Vallée de la Mort)». (USA)

■148, 149 «Ambivalences du bleu», c'est ainsi que s'intitule l'article illustré de ces photos du photographe allemand Thomas Schmid dans le magazine HQ publié par les Machines à imprimer Heidelberger. (GER)

PHOTOGRAPHER:
ALAN GELLER
CLIENT:
ALAN GELLER
ART DIRECTOR:
ALAN GELLER
◄■ 147

PHOTOGRAPHER:
THOMAS SCHMID
PUBLISHER:
VERLAG HIGH QUALITY
CLIENT:
*HEIDELBERGER
DRUCKMASCHINEN AG*
ART DIRECTOR:
ROLF MÜLLER
AGENCY:
DESIGN BÜRO ROLF MÜLLER
►■ 148, 149

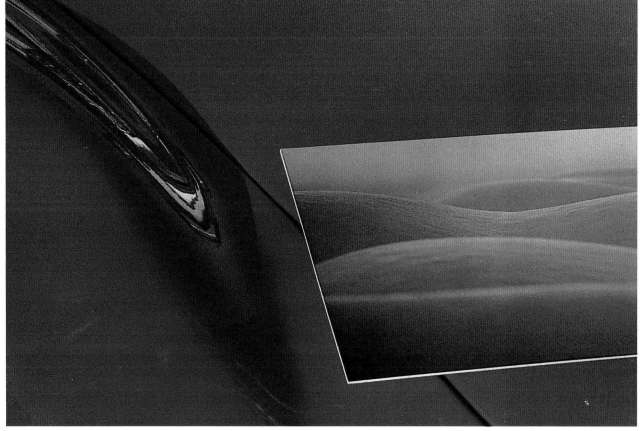

PHOTOGRAPHER:
HANS VERHUFEN
PUBLISHER:
INTERNATIONAL PUBLISHING CORP.
BIRKHÄUSER VERLAG
ART DIRECTOR:
PETER WONG
DESIGNER:
ALBERT GOMM
■ 150

■ 150, 151 Double spreads from the book "China – World Famous Photographers on the Track of the Long March" published by Birkhäuser Verlag. Shown on the left page is a shot of a steam locomotive pulling a freight train from which liquid waste containers are unloaded. It was taken by Hans Verhufen on location near Dukou, an important center of China's iron and steel industry. Gregory Heisler's photo (right page) was taken at the Qingsheixang Lake in Yongsheng. The sun suddenly broke through to illuminate the precisely arranged fields. (SWI)

■ 150, 151 Aus dem im Birkhäuser Verlag erschienenen Buch *China – Weltbekannte Photographen auf den Spuren des Langen Marsches*. Links eine Aufnahme von Hans Verhufen, die einen von einer Dampflokomotive angetriebenen Güterzug zeigt, aus dessen Containern Flüssigschlacke entladen wird. Sie entstand in der Nähe von Dukou, einem wichtigen Zentrum der Eisen- und Stahlindustrie Chinas. Gregory Heislers Photo (rechte Seite) entstand am Qingsheixang-See in Yongsheng: die plötzlich durchbrechende Sonne beleuchtet die präzise angelegten Felder. (SWI)

■ 150, 151 Doubles pages de l'ouvrage «La Chine – des photographes de renommée mondiale sur les traces de la Longue Marche», paru aux Editions Birkhäuser. Sur la photo à gauche de Hans Verhufen, un train de marchandises à vapeur décharge du laitier de coulée près de Dukou, un centre sidérurgique important. La photo de Gregory Heisler (page de droite) a été réalisée sur les rives du lac Qingsheixang à Yongsheng; les rayons du soleil traversant les nuages illuminent le tracé régulier des champs disposés avec précision. (SWI)

PHOTOGRAPHER:
Gregory Heisler
PUBLISHER:
International Publishing Corp.
Birkhäuser Verlag
ART DIRECTOR:
Peter Wong
DESIGNER:
Albert Gomm
■ 151

PHOTOGRAPHER:
KURT MARKUS
CLIENT:
US WEST INC.
ART DIRECTOR:
PAT BURNHAM
DESIGNER:
FALLON MCELLIGOTT
STUDIO:
KURT MARKUS LTD.
■ 152-154

■ 152-154 Photographs for
the January, August and
February sheets of a calendar issued by *U.S. West.*
They were taken in the
American West and convey
a spirit of wildness and ad-
venture that in these regions
is still not quite lost. (USA)

■ 152-154 Aufnahmen für
das Januar-, August- und
Februarblatt eines Kalenders
von *U.S. West,* entstanden
im Westen der USA. Sie ver-
mitteln ein Gefühl von Wild-
heit und Abenteuer, das hier
noch nicht ganz verloren-
ging. (USA)

■ 152-154 Photos illustrant
les feuillets de janvier, d'août
et de février d'un calendrier
d'*U.S. West.* Elles ont toutes été réalisées dans l'Ouest
des Etats-Unis, dont elles
traduisent le caractère sau-
vage et aventureux irrem-
plaçable. (USA)

PHOTOGRAPHER:
ROBERT DOWLING
CLIENT:
SINGAPORE AIRLINES
ART DIRECTOR:
GRAHAM BYFIELD
DESIGNER:
GRAHAM BYFIELD
AGENCY:
BATEY ADS
■155, 156

■155, 156 Photographs for an advertising campaign for *Singapore Airlines*. The headlines read: "Venice, not an easy place to leave" and "Montmartre can be chilly around daybreak" – as a consolation the flight home with *Singapore Airlines*. (SIN)

■155, 156 Aufnahmen aus einer Werbekampagne für *Singapore Airlines*. «Venedig, ein Ort von dem man sich schwer trennt» und «Montmartre kann bei Tagesanbruch sehr kühl sein» – als Trost wird hier der Heimflug mit *Singapore Airlines* angepriesen. (SIN)

■155, 156 Photos pour une campagne de la compagnie aérienne *Singapore Airlines*. «Venise, un endroit qu'on quitte à regret»; «Montmartre, un endroit qui peut être glacial aux petites heures du jour» – heureusement, il y a le retour par *Singapore Airlines*. (SIN)

PHOTOGRAPHER:
Tim Bieber
CLIENT:
Tim Bieber Photography
DESIGNER:
Steve Liska
■ 157, 158

■ 157, 158 Iceland and New
Buffalo, Michigan – photographs by Tim Bieber from
a diary. (USA)

■ 157, 158 Island und New
Buffalo, Michigan – Aufnah-
men aus einer Agenda mit
Photos von Tim Bieber. (USA)

■ 157, 158 L'Islande et New
Buffalo dans le Michigan –
photos d'un agenda illustré
par Tim Bieber. (USA)

PHOTOGRAPHER:
JOHN CLARIDGE
PUBLISHER:
ZOOM:
CLIENT:
JOHN CLARIDGE
ART DIRECTOR:
JOHN CLARIDGE
■159

■159 Photograph from
a special issue of *Zoom*
on photographers repre-
sented by the *Image
Bank.* London photog-
rapher John Claridge
doesn't only document
reality, but also renders
beauty. (FRA)

■159 Aus einer Sonder-
nummer von *Zoom* über die
von *Image Bank* vertrete-
nen Photographen. Der
Londoner John Claridge
dokumentiert nicht die
Wirklichkeit, sondern arran-
giert seine Aufnahmen zu
schönen Bildern. (FRA)

■159 Photo figurant dans
un numéro spécial de *Zoom*
consacré aux photographes
représentés par *Image
Bank.* Le Londonien John
Claridge ne documente pas
le réel, mais compose ses
photos de manière à les
rendre belles. (FRA)

PHOTOGRAPHER:
RON BAMBRIDGE
■ 160, 161

■ 160, 161 Personal studies by British photographer Ron Bambridge taken in North Wales and presented in the book *Best of British*, Rotovision, Geneva. (SWI)

■ 160, 161 In North Wales entstandene, persönliche Studien des britischen Photographen Ron Bambridge, vorgestellt in dem Buch *Best of British*, Rotovision Genf. (SWI)

■ 160, 161 Etudes personnelles de Ron Bambridge réalisées dans le nord du pays de Galles et présentées dans l'ouvrage *Best of British* (Rotovision, Genève). (SWI)

PHOTOGRAPHER:
GARY BRAASCH
CLIENT:
HARDING LAWSON ASSOCIATES
DESIGNER:
MICHAEL MANWARING
■ 162-164

■ 162-164 Full-page photographs from a company brochure for Harding Lawson Associates, a group of engineers and geoscientists engaged in geophysical techniques and environmental services. (USA)

■ 162-164 Ganzseitige Aufnahmen aus einer Firmenbroschüre für Harding Lawson Associates, ein Unternehmen, das sich mit geophysikalischen Techniken und umwelttechnischen Belangen befasst. (USA)

■ 162-164 Photos pleine page illustrant une brochure publicitaire de Harding Lawson Associates, une entreprise spécialisée dans les techniques géophysiques et les problèmes techniques relatifs à la protection de l'environnement. (USA)

Photographer:
Roger Chappellu
Publisher:
Editions Olizane
Art Director:
Olivier Lombard
Designer:
Roger Chappellu
■ 165, 166

■ 165, 166 Photograph for the cover of the photo book *Genève* (Editions Olizane, Geneva) and an illustration from its contents. The shots are by photographer Roger Chappellu. Shown is the mirror-image of the city on a terrace and a reflection of a crane, route de Frontenex. (SWI)

■ 165, 166 Umschlagphoto des Buches *Genève* (Editions Olizane, Genf) und eine Abbildung aus dem Inhalt dieses Bildbandes mit Aufnahmen des Photographen Roger Chappellu. Hier das Spiegelbild der Stadt auf einer Terrasse und die Spiegelung eines Krans, route de Frontenex. (SWI)

■ 165, 166 Photo de couverture de l'ouvrage *Genève* paru aux Editions Olizane de Genève et illustration figurant dans cet album qui est l'œuvre du photographe Roger Chappellu. On voit ici la silhouette de la ville se refléter depuis la terrasse du Seujet et le reflet d'un grue, route de Frontenex. (SWI)

ARCHITECTURE

ARCHITECTURE

ARCHITEKTUR

ARCHITECTURE

PHOTOGRAPHER:
BRUCE WOLF
CLIENT:
MARTEX/WEST POINT PEPPERELL
ART DIRECTOR:
JAMES SEBASTIAN
DESIGNER:
JAMES SEBASTIAN/
WILLIAM WALTER
AGENCY:
DESIGNFRAME INC.
■ 167, 168

■ 167, 168 Photograph for the cover and a further shot from the contents of a catalogue for *Martex* home textiles, entitled "Special Rooms" – chosen here as effective ambience for the textiles. (USA)

■ 169 Cover of a self-promotional brochure for the architect team Leason Pomeroy Associates. (USA)

■ 167, 168 Aufnahme für den Umschlag und ein weiteres Photo aus dem Inhalt eines Kataloges für *Martex*-Heimtextilien, unter dem Titel »besondere Räume« – hier als wirkungsvolle Umgebung für die Textilien ausgewählt. (USA)

■ 169 Umschlag einer Eigenwerbungsbroschüre des Architekten-Teams Leason Pomeroy Associates. (USA)

■ 167, 168 Illustration de couverture et une autre photo tirée d'un catalogue des tissus d'intérieur *Martex* intitulé «Espaces particuliers» par référence aux décors prestigieux choisis pour la présentation de ces textiles. (USA)

■ 169 Couverture d'une brochure autopromotionnelle du bureau d'architecture Leason Pomeroy Associates. (USA)

PHOTOGRAPHER:
CHARLY FRANKLIN
CLIENT:
LEASON POMEROY ASSOCIATES
ART DIRECTOR:
MICHAEL MANWARING
DESIGNER:
MICHAEL MANWARING
AGENCY:
MICHAEL MANWARING
■ 169

PHOTOGRAPHER:
KLAUS P. OHLENFORST
CLIENT:
HENKEL KGAA
ART DIRECTOR:
MICHAEL KARSULKE
DESIGNER:
MICHAEL KARSULKE
AGENCY:
TBWA SPEZIAL GMBH
■ 170–172

PHOTOGRAPHER:
FRÉDÉRIC KLEIN
CLIENT:
THREE H MANUFACTURING LTD.
ART DIRECTOR:
FRÉDÉRIC KLEIN
STUDIO:
STUDIO 70
■ 173

■ 170-172 Photographs for an ad campaign in magazines, for the chemical firm of *Henkel.* (GER)

■ 173 Photograph from a promotional brochure for furniture made by Three H Manufacturing Ltd. (CAN)

■ 170-172 Aufnahmen für eine Anzeigenkampagne in Zeitschriften für den Chemiekonzern *Henkel.* (GER)

■ 173 Aufnahme aus einer Werbebroschüre für Möbel der Firma Three H Manufacturing Ltd. (CAN)

■ 170-172 Photos utilisées pour une campagne d'annonces de magazines de groupe chimique *Henkel.* (GER)

■ 173 Photo tirée d'une brochure publicitaire des Ameublements Three H Manufacturing Ltd. (CAN)

PHOTOGRAPHER:
BRUCE WOLF
CLIENT:
MARTEX/WEST POINT PEPPERELL
ART DIRECTOR:
JAMES SEBASTIAN
DESIGNER:
JAMES SEBASTIAN/WILLIAM WALTER
AGENCY:
DESIGNFRAME INC.
■ 174-178

■ 174-178 Examples of the double-spread photographs from a large-format catalogue for home textiles by *Martex* of West Point Pepperell. (USA)

■ 174-178 Beispiele der doppelseitigen Aufnahmen aus einem grossformatigen Katalog für Heimtextilien der Marke *Martex* von West Point Pepperell. (USA)

■ 174-178 Exemples des photos double page illustrant un catalogue au grand format des tissus d'intérieur *Martex*, publié par West Point Pepperell. (USA)

PHOTOGRAPHER:
RICHARD MANDELKORN
CLIENT:
TARGET PRODUCTIONS
ART DIRECTOR:
STEPHANIE HODEL
STUDIO:
*MANDELKORN ARCHITECTURAL
PHOTOGRAPHY*
■ 179

■ 179 Photograph of a conference room – from an advertising brochure for Target Productions, Inc., a video and post-production facility headquartered in Boston. (USA)

■ 180, 181 Meeting place and devotion room of the Shaker sect and some of the objects made by its members. The Shakers' handicrafts are renowned for the simplicity of design and quality of finish. (USA)

■ 179 Konferenzraum – aus einer Werbebroschüre der Target Productions, Inc., einer auf Video-Produktionen spezialisierten Firma in der Nähe von Boston. (USA)

■ 180, 181 Als Versammlungs- und Andachtsort bestimmter Raum der Shaker-Sekte und die von Angehörigen dieser Sekte gefertigten Gegenstände, die sich durch schlichtes Design und handwerkliche Qualität auszeichnen. (USA)

■ 179 Salle de conférences reproduite dans une brochure publicitaire de Target Productions, Inc., société de production vidéo et de marketing dont le siège est à Boston. (USA)

■ 180, 181 Local utilisé pour les assemblées et veillées de prières de la secte des Shakers, et photos montrant les travaux artisanaux réalisés par les membres de la secte; le design en est sobre, la qualité artisanale remarquable. (USA)

PHOTOGRAPHER:
Michael Melford/
Wheeler Pictures
PUBLISHER:
Travel & Leisure Magazine
ART DIRECTOR:
Adrian Taylor
■ 180, 181

PHOTOGRAPHER:
STEVE ROSENTHAL
CLIENT:
BOSTON DESIGN CENTER
■ 182

■ 182 Photograph of the Boston Design Center from the magazine *House & Garden.* A former army warehouse and coincidentally the world's largest building from 1917-1944, the Boston Design Center has captured several awards for adaptive reuse or restauration. The facade appears small but the building extents backward for over 500 yards. (USA)

■ 182 Aufnahme aus *House & Garden.* Das Boston Design Center hat für Renovationsarbeiten an diesem Gebäude, welches von 1917-1944 als grösstes Gebäude der Welt galt und ursprünglich als Armee-Lagerhaus benutzt wurde, verschiedene Auszeichnungen erhalten. Die Grösse der Fassade täuscht: das Gebäude ist über 500 m lang. (USA)

■ 182 Photo du Boston Design Center, dans le magazine *House & Garden.* Cet ancien arsenal militaire, qui a été de 1917 à 1944 le plus grand bâtiment du monde, a été signalé à plusieurs reprises à l'attention publique par les prix décernés aux architectes qui l'ont restauré. La façade est moins large que le bâtiment n'est long (plus de 500 m). (USA)

PEOPLE

MENSCHEN

PERSONNES

PHOTOGRAPHER:
ROBERT MAPPLETHORPE
AGENCY:
ART + COMMERCE
■ 183, 184

■ 183, 184 Lucy Ferry, 1987; Laurie Anderson, 1987 – portrait shots by Robert Mapplethorpe. (USA)

■ 183, 184 Lucy Ferry, 1987; Laurie Anderson, 1987 – Porträtaufnahmen von Robert Mapplethorpe. (USA)

■ 183, 184 Lucy Ferry, 1987; Laurie Anderson, 1987 – portraits noir et blanc de Robert Mapplethorpe. (USA)

PHOTOGRAPHER:
ABE FRAJNDLICH
PUBLISHER:
FRANKFURTER ALLGEMEINE
ZEITUNG GMBH
ART DIRECTOR:
HANS-GEORG POSPISCHIL
■ 187

■ 187 Photograph for the introductory double spread to an article about Roy Lichtenstein, famed for being the father of Pop Art. From the *Frankfurter Allgemeine Magazin.* (GER)

■ 188 From a series of portrait photographs of English painters which photographer Evelyn Hofer was commissioned to take for the magazine *Vanity Fair;* shown is a portrait of Howard Hodgkin. (USA)

■ 189 Portrait of Italian author Alberto Moravia, taken by Toni Thorimbert within a feature entitled "Other Views of Italy", appearing in *Camera International.* (FRA)

■ 187 Einleitende Doppelseite zu einem Artikel über Roy Lichtenstein, der als einer der Väter der Pop Art berühmt wurde. Aus dem *Frankfurter Allgemeine Magazin.* (GER)

■ 188 Aus einer Reihe von Porträtaufnahmen, die die Photographin Evelyn Hofer ursprünglich im Auftrag des Magazins *Vanity Fair* von englischen Malern machte; hier Howard Hodgkin. (USA)

■ 189 Porträt des italienischen Schriftstellers Alberto Moravia von Toni Thorimbert. Aus einem Beitrag mit dem Titel «Andere Ansichten von Italien» in *Camera International.* (FRA)

■ 187 La double page initiale d'un article du *Frankfurter Allgemeine Magazin* consacré à Roy Lichtenstein, qui accéda à la célébrité comme l'un des pères du pop art. (GER)

■ 188 Exemple d'une série de portraits d'artistes peintres anglais que la photographe Evelyn Hofer réalisa à l'origine en 1984 pour le compte du magazine *Vanity Fair;* ici: Howard Hodgkin. (USA)

■ 189 Portrait de l'écrivain italien Alberto Moravia par Toni Thorimbert. Il a illustré un article de *Camera International* intitulé «D'autres regards sur l'Italie». (FRA)

PHOTOGRAPHER:
EVELYN HOFER
PUBLISHER:
U.S. EYE PUBLISHING CO.
ART DIRECTOR:
ANTHONY RUSSELL
DESIGNER:
CASEY CLARK
AGENCY:
ANTHONY RUSSELL INC.
■ 188

PHOTOGRAPHER:
TONI THORIMBERT
PUBLISHER:
RIZZOLI AMICA/
CAMERA INTERNATIONAL
ART DIRECTOR:
GIOVANNA CALVENZI/
GABRIEL BAURET
■ 189

PHOTOGRAPHER:
ROLPH GOBITS
CLIENT:
MORGAN GRENFELL
ART DIRECTOR:
AZIZ CAMI
DESIGNER:
SHAUN DEW
AGENCY:
THE PARTNERS
■ 190–194

■ 190-194 Portrait photographs of leading employees of the international banking corporation Morgan Grenfell, for a promotion portfolio. The employees, based overseas, were photographed in the majority of cases against a background typical of the region, *190:* Hongkong, *193:* Sydney. (GBR)

■ 190-194 Porträtaufnahmen von leitenden Angestellten der international tätigen Bank-Gruppe Morgan Grenfell, für eine Promotionsmappe. Die im Ausland tätigen Mitarbeiter wurden in den meisten Fällen vor einem für den Ort typischen Hintergrund aufgenommen, *190:* Hongkong, *193:* Sidney. (GBR)

■ 190-194 Portraits de cadres supérieurs de groupe bancaire international Morgan Grenfell, pour un dossier publicitaire. La plupart des cadres travaillant à l'étranger ont été photographiés dans un décor national typique, *190:* Hongkong et *193:* Sydney. (GBR)

■ 195 "View from the White House" – photograph for the promotional calendar of a printing company. (USA)

■ 196 From a series of portraits of the American working class photographed for an advertising campaign by Seagram's Distillers. (USA)

■ 195 «Ausblick vom Weissen Haus» – Aufnahme für den Werbekalender einer Druckerei. (USA)

■ 196 Aus einer Serie von Porträts der amerikanischen Arbeiterklasse für eine Anzeigenkampagne von Seagram's Distillers. (USA)

■ 195 «Vue depuis la Maison-Blanche» – photo illustrant le calendrier publicitaire d'un imprimeur. (USA)

■ 196 Exemple d'une série de portraits du monde ouvrier américain utilisée pour une campagne d'annonces de Seagram's Distillers. (USA)

PHOTOGRAPHER:
LARRY OLSEN
CLIENT:
STEPHENSON, INC.
ART DIRECTOR:
JOHN MICHAEL
DESIGNER:
JOHN MICHAEL
AGENCY:
ADAMS STUDIO
■ 195

PHOTOGRAPHER:
JAMES SALZANO
CLIENT:
SEAGRAM'S DISTILLERS, INC.
ART DIRECTOR:
PAUL SCOLARO
DESIGNER:
PAUL SCOLARO
AGENCY:
OGILVY & MATHER
■ 196

PHOTOGRAPHER:
WOLFGANG WESENER

PUBLISHER:
*FRANKFURTER ALLGEMEINE
ZEITUNG GMBH*

ART DIRECTOR:
HANS-GEORG POSPISCHIL

■ 197, 198

PHOTOGRAPHER:
JEAN-PAUL GOUDE

PUBLISHER:
*ART DIRECTORS CLUB
VERLAG GMBH*

ART DIRECTOR:
HELMUT ROTTKE

► ■ 199

■ 197, 198 Full-page photographs from a feature in the *Frankfurter Allgemeine Magazin* on Keith Haring, the "man of the moment" on the New York art scene. (GER)

■ 199 Cover photograph of the 1987 yearbook of the Art Directors Club of Germany. (GER)

■ 197, 198 Ganzseitige Aufnahmen aus einem Beitrag im *Frankfurter Allgemeine Magazin* über Keith Haring, den «Mann der Minute» der New Yorker Kunstszene. (GER)

■ 199 Umschlagphoto des Jahrbuches 1987 des Art Directors Club für Deutschland. (GER)

■ 197, 198 Photos illustrant un article que le *Frankfurter Allgemeine Magazin* consacre à Keith Haring, «la vedette de la minute» de la scène artistique new-yorkaise. (GER)

■ 199 Photo de couverture de l'annuel 1987 de l'Art Directors Club ouest-allemand. (GER)

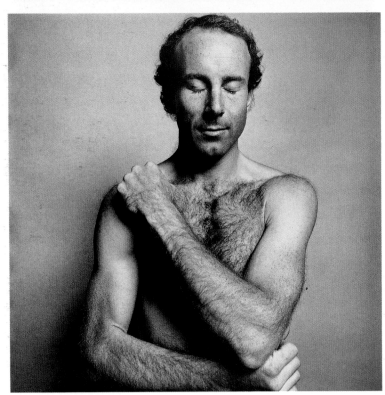

PHOTOGRAPHER:
TERRY O'NEILL
▲
▲■ 200

PHOTOGRAPHER:
HANS GEDDA
▲■ 202

PHOTOGRAPHER:
DICK ZIMMERMAN
▲
▲■ 201

PHOTOGRAPHER:
PATRICK JACOB
▲
▲■ 203

PHOTOGRAPHER:
BEN OYNE
■ 204

CLIENT:
HASSELBLAD SVENSKA AB
ART DIRECTOR:
STYRBJORN LYBERG
DESIGNER:
LARS OHJNE
AGENCY:
OHJNE & CO.
■ 200-204

■ 200-204 Portrait photographs from an ad campaign for *Hasselblad* cameras. Shown are Faye Dunaway, Jane Seymour, Ingemar Stenmark, Karl Lagerfeld and Paul Bocuse, taken by various photographers. (SWE)

■ 200-204 Porträtaufnahmen aus einer Anzeigenkampagne für *Hasselblad*-Kameras. Hier Faye Dunaway, Jane Seymour, Ingemar Stenmark, Karl Lagerfeld und Paul Bocuse, aufgenommen von verschiedenen Photographen. (SWE)

■ 200-204 Portraits utilisés pour une campagne d'annonces des appareils photo *Hasselblad:* Faye Dunaway, Jane Seymour, Ingemar Stenmark, Karl Lagerfeld et Paul Bocuse interprétés par divers photographes. (SWE)

PHOTOGRAPHER:
WOLFGANG WESENER
PUBLISHER:
*FRANKFURTER ALLGEMEINE
ZEITUNG GMBH*
ART DIRECTOR:
HANS-GEORG POSPISCHIL
DESIGNER:
BERNADETTE GOTTHARDT
■ 205

PHOTOGRAPHER:
RICHARD AVEDON
COPYRIGHT © 1985 BY
RICHARD AVEDON INC.
ALL RIGHTS RESERVED.
PUBLISHER:
NICOLE WISNIAK
ART DIRECTOR:
NICOLE WISNIAK
►■ 206

■ 205 Andy Warhol in front of a self-portrait. Photograph
for the introductory double spread of a feature about this
artist in the *Frankfurter Allgemeine Magazin.* (GER)

■ 206 Self-portrait of photographer Richard Avedon taken
on August 20, 1980, in Provo, Utah. (USA)

■ 205 Andy Warhol vor einem Selbstporträt - Aufnahme
für die einleitende Doppelseite zu einem Beitrag über diesen
Künstler im *Frankfurter Allgemeine Magazin.* (GER)

■ 206 Selbstporträt des Photographen Richard Avedon, welches am 20. August 1980 in Provo, Utah, entstand. (USA)

■ 205 Andy Warhol devant son autoportrait - photo desti-
née à la première double page d'un article que lui consacre
le *Frankfurter Allgemeine Magazin.* (GER)

■ 206 Autoportrait du photographe Richard Avedon pris le
20 août 1980 à Provo, Utah. (USA)

PHOTOGRAPHER:
PIOTR TOPPERZER
CLIENT:
CAFÉ VICTOR
DESIGNER:
CLAUS MUNCK
AGENCY:
PIOTR & CO.
■ 207, 208

■ 207, 208 Black-and-white photographs from the jubilee brochure of a cafe, with portraits of all employees. (DEN)

■ 209-211 Personal studies taken by photographer Franck Brunel of Paris. (FRA)

■ 212-214 "Incognito" is the title of these photographs used as self-promotion for photographer Rodney Rascona. (USA)

■ 207, 208 Schwarzweissaufnahmen aus der Jubiläumsbroschüre eines Cafés mit Porträts aller Angestellten. (DEN)

■ 209-211 Persönliche Studien des Photographen Franck Brunel, Paris. (FRA)

■ 212-214 «Incognito» - Aufnahmen, die der Photograph Rodney Rascona als Eigenwerbung verwendete. (USA)

■ 207, 208 Photos noir et blanc pour la brochure jubiliaire d'un café illustrée des portraits de ses employés. (DEN)

■ 209-211 Etudes personnelles réalisées par le photographe parisien Franck Brunel. (FRA)

■ 212-214 Ces photos, sous le titre d'«Incognito», servent à l'autopromotion du photographe Rodney Rascona. (USA)

PHOTOGRAPHER:
FRANCK BRUNEL
STUDIO:
FRANCK BRUNEL
■ 209-211

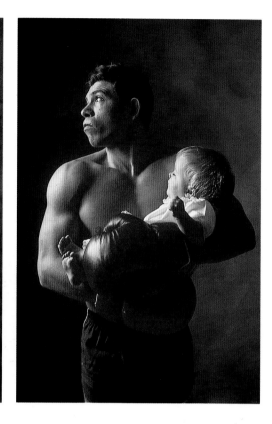

PHOTOGRAPHER:
RODNEY RASCONA
CLIENT:
RASCONA STUDIO
ART DIRECTOR:
RODNEY RASCONA
■ 212-214

PHOTOGRAPHER:
HERB RITTS
PUBLISHER:
SIRE RECORDS CO.
CLIENT:
MADONNA
ART DIRECTOR:
JERI MCMANUS-HEIDEN/
JEFF AYEROFF
DESIGNER:
JERI MCMANUS-HEIDEN
AGENCY:
WARNER BROS. RECORDS, INC.
■ 215

PHOTOGRAPHER:
WILLIAM COUPON
PUBLISHER:
DE GEILLUSTREERDE PERS B.V.
ART DIRECTOR:
HANS VAN BLOMMESTEIN
■ 216

PHOTOGRAPHER:
FRÉDÉRIC HUIJBREGTS
CLIENT:
VOGUE HOMME
PUBLISHER:
CONDÉ NAST SA
ART DIRECTOR:
FRÉDÉRIC HUIJBREGTS
■ 217

■ 215 Madonna - photograph for a record sleeve published by Warner Bros. Records, Inc. (USA)

■ 216 Portrait of pop singer Mick Jagger, from an article in the magazine *Avenue*. (NLD)

■ 217 Self-promotion for photographer Frédéric Huijbregts who specializes in portraits. Shown is Karl Lagerfeld. (FRA)

■ 215 Madonna - Aufnahme für die Hülle einer bei Warner Bros. Records, Inc. erschienenen Schallplatte. (USA)

■ 216 Porträt von Rock-Star Mick Jagger, aus einem Artikel in der Zeitschrift *Avenue*. (NLD)

■ 217 Eigenwerbung des auf Porträts spezialisierten Photographen Frédéric Huijbregts, hier Karl Lagerfeld. (FRA)

■ 215 Madonna - photo pour la pochette d'un disque produit par Warner Bros. Records, Inc. (USA)

■ 216 Portrait de la star du rock Mick Jagger, pour un article du magazine *Avenue*. (NLD)

■ 217 Autopromotion du photographe portraitiste Frédéric Huijbregts: Karl Lagerfeld. (FRA)

PHOTOGRAPHER:
SERGE COHEN
PUBLISHER:
*FRANKFURTER ALLGEMEINE
ZEITUNG GMBH*
ART DIRECTOR:
HANS-GEORG POSPISCHIL
DESIGNER:
BERNADETTE GOTTHARDT
■ 218, 219

PHOTOGRAPHER:
Wolfgang Wesener
PUBLISHER:
Frankfurter Allgemeine Zeitung GmbH
ART DIRECTOR:
Hans-Georg Pospischil
DESIGNER:
Bernadette Gotthardt
■ 220

■ 218, 219 Photographer Alfred Eisenstaedt is portrayed in front of a small selection of his photos and in the midst of yellow boxes full of his archive photographs. Serge Cohen photographed the doyen of photography for an article appearing in the *Frankfurter Allgemeine Magazin*. (GER)

■ 220 Double-spread photograph from a feature in the *Frankfurter Allgemeine Magazin* on the now much calmer rock star Frank Zappa. (GER)

■ 218, 219 Der Photograph Alfred Eisenstaedt vor einer kleinen Auswahl seiner Bilder und inmitten seiner in zahlreichen gelben Kartons archivierten Photos. Serge Cohen photographierte den Altmeister der Photographie für einen Artikel im *Frankfurter Allgemeine Magazin*. (GER)

■ 220 Doppelseitige Aufnahme aus einem Beitrag im *Frankfurter Allgemeine Magazin* über den inzwischen etwas ruhiger gewordenen Rockstar Frank Zappa. (GER)

■ 218, 219 Le photographe Alfred Eisenstaedt devant une sélection de ses œuvres; tout autour, ses archives photo classées dans de nombreux cartons jaunes. Serge Cohen a pris sur le vif le maître de la photographie de jadis, pour un article du *Frankfurter Allgemeine Magazin*. (GER)

■ 220 Photo double page pour un article du *Frankfurter Allgemeine Magazin* où il est question de la vedette du rock Frank Zappa dont l'étoile a quelque peu faibli. (GER)

■ 221-225 Photographs from an article on the people of Afghanistan, in the magazine *Moda*. Only this woman's foot is visible, and the photographer had to wait three weeks for the shot, since Afghanistanis are convinced that the camera is able to see through clothes. He took the shot in secret – at the risk of being stoned. All photographs were taken in a camp: partisans, an old woman with her grandchild (in Afghanistan only old women and widows are allowed to show their face uncovered) and a shepherd. (ITA)

■ 221-225 Aus einem Artikel über die Menschen in Afghanistan, in der Zeitschrift *Moda*. Für diese Aufnahme einer Frau musste der Photograph 3 Wochen warten, weil die Afghanen überzeugt sind, dass die Kamera durch die Kleider sehen kann. Er machte die Aufnahme heimlich und riskierte dabei, gesteinigt zu werden. Alle Aufnahmen entstanden in einem Lager: Partisanen, eine alte Frau mit ihrem Enkel (nur alte Frauen und Witwen dürfen ihr Gesicht unverhüllt zeigen) und ein Schäfer. (ITA)

■ 221-225 D'un article du magazine *Moda* sur la vie des gens en Afghanistan. Le photographe a dû attendre trois semaines pour gagner la confiance des villageois qui croyaient que la photo pouvait traverser les vêtements, alors que seul le pied de la femme est visible. Finalement il prit cette photo en cachette, risquant la lapidation. Les photos proviennent d'un camp de la résistance. On y voit des partisans, une vieille femme (non voilée comme toutes celles de son âge et les veuves) avec son petit-fils, un berger. (ITA)

PHOTOGRAPHER:
JULIO DONOSO/SYGMA
PUBLISHER:
ERI EDIZIONI RAI
ART DIRECTOR:
STUDIO SERGIO SARTORI
■ 221-225

■ 226 Group photo of the third Infantry RS-6 Company, from a special issue of the *Schweizer Illustrierte* entitled "A Day in the Life of Switzerland" showing 75 photos by 75 photographers. (SWI)

■ 227 Double-spread photograph from the book "China – World Famous Photographers on the Track of the Long March" published by Birkhäuser Verlag. Shown are recruits of the People's Freedom Army, who now, in contrast to former times, have new uniforms as well as better education. (SWI)

■ 226 Gruppenbild der 3. Kompanie der Infanterie-RS 6, aus einer Sondernummer der *Schweizer Illustrierten* unter dem Motto «Ein Tag im Leben der Schweiz» mit 75 Aufnahmen von 75 Photographen. (SWI)

■ 227 Doppelseitige Aufnahme aus dem im Birkhäuser Verlag erschienenen Buch *China – Weltbekannte Photographen auf den Spuren des Langen Marsches:* Rekruten der Volksbefreiungsarmee, die gegenüber früher nicht nur eine neue Uniform, sondern auch eine bessere Schulbildung haben. (SWI)

■ 226 Photo de groupe de la 3e compagnie de l'Ecole de recrues d'infanterie 6, dans un numéro spécial du *Schweizer Illustrierte:* «Une journée de la vie de la Suisse», reportage en 75 photos de 75 photographes. (SWI)

■ 227 Photo double page tirée de l'ouvrage *China – Weltbekannte Photographen auf den Spuren des Langen Marsches* (Ed. Birkhäuser), où de grands photographes explorent la Chine «sur les traces de la Longue Marche»: recrues de l'armée de la libération populaire bénéficiant d'un nouvel uniforme et d'une meilleure éducation. (SWI)

Photographer:
Enrico Ferorelli
Publisher:
*Birkhäuser Verlag/
International Publishing*
Art Director:
Peter Wong
Designer:
Albert Gomm
■ 227

PHOTOGRAPHER:
GREGORY EDWARDS/
WHEELER PICTURES
CLIENT:
POTLATCH PAPER CORP.
ART DIRECTOR:
KEVIN B. KUESTER
DESIGNER:
MADSEN & KUESTER
■ 228-235

■ 228-235 Photographs taken by Gregory Edwards at the Minneapolis state fair for paper producer *Potlatch*. From left to right: accordion player from a polka band; punk rockers; marching band musician; snake handler with python; boy with duck; "Miss Rodeo Queen"; poultry judging show; "Guess your Weight". (USA)

■ 228-235 Bei einem Markt im Staat Minneapolis entstandene Aufnahmen für den Papierhersteller *Potlatch*. Von links nach rechts: Akkordeon-Spieler einer Polka-Gruppe; Punks; Mitglied einer Marschkapelle; Schlangenbändiger mit einer Python; Junge mit Ente; «Miss Rodeo Queen»; bei der Geflügelausstellung; «Schätze Dein Gewicht». (USA)

■ 228-235 Photos de foire, dans le Minneapolis, fief du fabricant de papier *Potlatch*. De gauche à droite: accordéonistes d'un orchestre de polka; punks; membres d'une fanfare; charmeur de serpents avec son python; garçon avec son canard; «Miss Rodéo Queen»; exposition de volailles; estimation du poids des visiteurs. (USA)

■ 236 Black-and-white photograph from an article on the subject of "Twins" in the Norwegian magazine *Tique*. (NOR)

■ 237 Portrait of the well-known American boxer "Marvellous Marvin" Hagler. (USA)

■ 236 Schwarzweissaufnahme aus einem Artikel über «Zwillinge» in der norwegischen Zeitschrift *Tique*. (NOR)

■ 237 Porträt des als «Marvellous Marvin» bekannten amerikanischen Boxers Marvin Hagler. (USA)

■ 236 Photo noir et blanc illustrant un article du magazine norvégien *Tique* où il est question de jumeaux. (NOR)

■ 237 Portrait du boxer américain Marvin Hagler, surnommé le Merveilleux (Marvellous Marvin). (USA)

PHOTOGRAPHER:
ANN LINDBERG
PUBLISHER:
TIQUE
ART DIRECTOR:
CECILIE WERGELAND
◄■ 236

PHOTOGRAPHER:
FRANK FOSTER
►■ 237

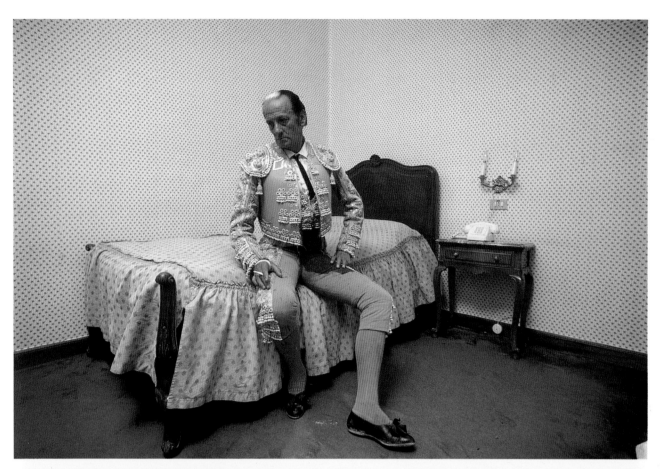

PHOTOGRAPHER:
SERGE COHEN
PUBLISHER:
*FRANKFURTER ALLGE-
MEINE ZEITUNG*
ART DIRECTOR:
HANS-GEORG POSPISCHIL
■ 238–240

■ 238–240 Photographs of Antoñete, one of the oldest and most adored of all Madrid's matadors, from a feature in the *Frankfurter Allgemeine Magazin.* (GER)

■ 238–240 Aufnahmen von Antoñete, einem der ältesten und beliebtesten Matadoren Madrids, aus einem Beitrag im *Frankfurter Allgemeine Magazin.* (GER)

■ 238–240 Photos d'Antoñete, l'un des matadors les plus chevronnés et les plus populaires de Madrid, dans un article du *Frankfurter Allgemeine Magazin.* (GER)

PHOTOGRAPHER:
ORION DAHLMANN
PUBLISHER:
VERLAG PHOTOGRAPHIE AG
ART DIRECTOR:
PETER WASSERMANN
DESIGNER:
ORION DAHLMANN
■ 241

■ 241 One of a series of portrait shots taken by photographer Orion Dahlmann, whose unconventional techniques create surrealistic moods. From a feature in *Portfolio Photographie.* (SWI)

■ 242 Photograph from the book *The Mexico of Sergio Bustamante.* Clint Clemens shot the sculptures by this Mexican artist. The photo was also used on the cover of the book. (USA)

■ 241 Beispiel aus einer Serie von Porträtaufnahmen des Photographen Orion Dahlmann, der mit unkonventionellen Techniken surreale Stimmungen schafft. Aus einem Beitrag in *Portfolio Photographie.* (SWI)

■ 242 Aufnahme aus dem Buch *The Mexico of Sergio Bustamante.* Clint Clements photographierte die Skulpturen dieses mexikanischen Künstlers. Das Photo wurde auch für den Buchumschlag verwendet. (USA)

■ 241 Exemple d'une série de portraits du photographe Orion Dahlmann réalisant une ambiance surréelle au moyen de techniques peu conventionnelles. D'un article dans *Portfolio Photographie.* (SWI)

■ 242 Photo tirée du livre *The Mexico of Sergio Bustamante.* C'est Clint Clemens qui a photographié les sculptures de cet artiste mexicain; illustration reprise pour la couverture. (USA)

PHOTOGRAPHER:
CLINT CLEMENS
CLIENT:
SERGIO BUSTAMANTE
DESIGNER:
TYLER SMITH
■ 242

Photographer:
Burkhard von Harder
◄■ 243

■ 243 "Man on the Diving Board" is the title of this shot by Hamburg photographer Burkhard von Harder. (GER)

■ 243 »Der Mann auf dem Sprungbrett« ist der Titel dieser Aufnahme des Hamburger Photographen Burkhard von Harder. (GER)

■ 243 Le photographe hambourgeois Burkhard von Harder a intitulé cette photo «L'homme sur le tremplin». (GER)

Photographer:
Jürgen Sieckmeyer
Publisher:
Edition Stemmle/
Verlag Photographie AG
Art Director:
Peter Wassermann
■ 244-246

■ 244-246 Photographs from the book "Peking Opera" published by Edition Stemmle. These photos show the interior of one of the small privately-run saloons – the only ones still remaining open after theater performances. (SWI)

■ 244-246 Aufnahmen aus dem Buch *Pekingoper*, erschienen bei Edition Stemmle. Diese Bilder zeigen das Innere eines der privat geführten kleinen Lokale, die als einzige nach den Theatervorstellungen noch geöffnet sind. (SWI)

■ 244-246 Photos tirées de *Pekingoper* (Opéra de Pékin), un ouvrage paru aux Editions Stemmle. On y voit l'intérieur de l'un des petits cafés qui restent seuls ouverts après le théâtre et qui sont des entreprises privées. (SWI)

PHOTOGRAPHER:
DOMINIQUE ISSERMANN
PUBLISHER:
SCHIRMER/MOSEL VERLAG
■ 247-251

■ 247-251 "The building is covered by such dense vegetation, that the light penetrates it only three days a year. On these three days I photographed Anne Rohart." This is the only text in the photo book *Anne Rohart* by Dominique Issermann, from which these black-and-white photographs are taken. Published by Schirmer/Mosel, Munich/Paris. (GER)

■ 247-251 «Den Bau verhüllt so dichte Vegetation, dass nur an drei Tagen im Jahr Licht einfällt. An diesen drei Tagen photographierte ich Anne Rohart.» Dies ist der einzige Text zu dem Photoband *Anne Rohart* von Dominique Issermann, aus dem diese Schwarzweissaufnahmen stammen. Verlag Schirmer/Mosel, München/Paris. (GER)

■ 247-251 «L'édifice est tellement masqué par une végétation si luxuriante qu'il ne reçoit de lumiere que trois jours par an. C'est pendant ces trois jours que j'ai photographié Anne Rohart.» Seule ligne de texte de l'album photo *Anne Rohart* de Dominique Issermann d'où sont tirés ces noir et blanc. Editions Schirmer/Mosel, Munich/Paris. (GER)

PHOTOGRAPHER:
TERENCE DONOVAN
CLIENT:
PIRELLI S.P.A.
◀■ 252

PHOTOGRAPHER:
FABRIZIO FERRI
PUBLISHER:
CAMERA INTERNATIONAL
ART DIRECTOR:
GABRIEL BAURET
■ 253, 254

■ 252 Photograph from one of the *Pirelli* calendars.
Photographer Terence Donovan chose five out of sixty
models from various regions of Africa. The shots were all
taken in the studio, the background was created with the
aid of a computer. (ITA)

■ 253, 254 From a series of black-and-white portrait photographs by Italian photographer Fabrizio Ferri, presented in
Camera International. (FRA)

■ 252 Aufnahme aus einem von *Pirelli* herausgegebenen
Kalender. Der Photograph Terence Donovan wählte unter
60 Bewerberinnen fünf Modelle aus verschiedenen Regionen
Afrikas aus. Die Aufnahmen entstanden im Studio, der Hintergrund wurde mit Hilfe eines Computers hergestellt. (ITA)

■ 253, 254 Beispiele aus einer Serie von schwarzweissen
Porträtaufnahmen des italienischen Photographen Fabrizio
Ferri, vorgestellt in *Camera International.* (FRA)

■ 252 Photo pour un calendrier publié par *Pirelli.* Le photographe anglais Terence Donovan dut sélectionner cinq
modèles parmi 60 candidates africaines. Les photos furent
réalisées en studio, avec simulation de l'arrière-plan par
ordinateur. (ITA)

■ 253, 254 Exemples d'une série de portraits noir et blanc
du photographe italien Fabrizio Ferri à laquelle *Camera International* consacre un article. (FRA)

PHOTOGRAPHER:
FRANÇOISE HUGUIER
CLIENT:
MARIE-CLAIRE BIS
AGENCY:
VU/CONTACT
■ 255–257

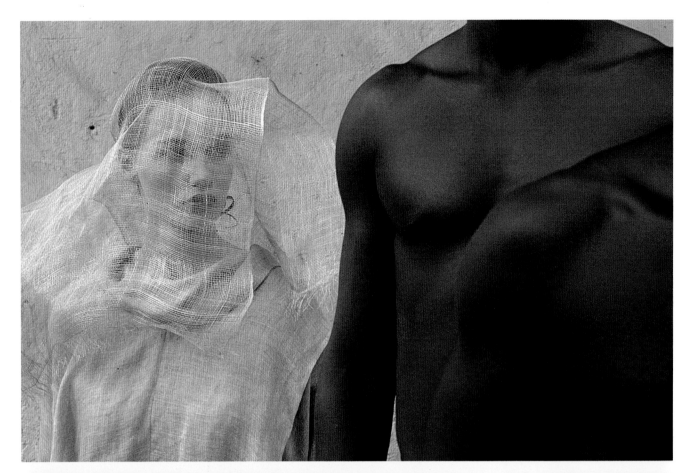

PHOTOGRAPHER:
FRANÇOISE HUGUIER
CLIENT:
MARIE-CLAIRE BIS
AGENCY:
VU/CONTACT

■ 255-257 From a series of photographs taken on location in Africa for the French magazine *Marie-Claire Bis.* (FRA)

■ 255-257 Aufnahmen aus einer Serie, die für die Zeitschrift *Marie-Claire Bis* in Afrika aufgenommen wurden. (FRA)

■ 255-257 Photos figurant dans une série realisée en Afrique pour le magazine français *Marie-Claire Bis.* (FRA)

PHOTOGRAPHER:
JOYCE TENNESON
■ 258–260

■ 258–260 From a series of personal work by the photographer Joyce Tenneson, exhibited at the Museum of Modern Art, Paris. (USA)

■ 258–260 Aus einer Serie persönlicher Arbeiten der Photographin Joyce Tenneson, ausgestellt im Musée national d'art moderne in Paris. (USA)

■ 258–260 Exemples des travaux personnels de la photographe Joyce Tenneson, exposés au Musée national d'art moderne de Paris. (USA)

PHOTOGRAPHER:
SHEILA METZNER
■ 261

PHOTOGRAPHER:
DAVID BAILEY
CLIENT:
VOGUE ITALIA
PUBLISHER:
CONDÉ NAST S.P.A.
ART DIRECTOR:
ALBERTO NODOLINI
■ 262

WILD LIFE

ANIMAUX

TIERE

ANIMAUX

■ 265 Double-spread shot from an article about photographer Frans Lanting in the magazine *Photography*. Shown are lesser flamingos on Lake Nakuru, Kenya. (GBR)

■ 266 Black-and-white photograph used for an exhibition poster for the Galérie Photo des Chiroux. (BEL)

■ 265 Doppelseitige Aufnahme aus der Zeitschrift *Photography*, aus einem Beitrag über den Photographen Frans Lanting. Hier Flamingos im Nakuru-See, Kenia. (GBR)

■ 266 Für ein Ausstellungsplakat des Photographen verwendete Schwarzweissaufnahme. (BEL)

■ 265 Photo double page parue dans le magazine *Photography*, dans un article consacré au photographe Frans Lanting: flamants au lac kenyan Nakuru. (GBR)

■ 266 Photo noir et blanc utilisée pour une affiche créée à l'occasion d'une exposition de l'œuvre du photographe. (BEL)

PHOTOGRAPHER:
FRANS LANTING
PUBLISHER:
PHOTOGRAPHY
DESIGNER:
KEITH LOVEGROVE
■ 265

PHOTOGRAPHER:
DANIEL MICHIELS
CLIENT:
GALÉRIE PHOTO DES CHIROUX
ART DIRECTOR:
JEAN-LUC DERU
DESIGNER:
JEAN-LUC DERU
AGENCY:
DAYLIGHT
■ 266

PHOTOGRAPHER:
CHRIS PACKHAM
■ 267

■ 267 "Study of a Dead Fish" – a shot by Chris Packham, winner of an award for composition and form by *Wildlife Photographers of the World.* (GBR)

■ 267 «Studie eines toten Fisches», eine von *Wildlife Photographers of the World* für Komposition und Form ausgezeichnete Aufnahme von Chris Packham. (GBR)

■ 267 «Etude d'un poisson mort» – photo de Chris Packham primée par l'organisation *Wildlife Photographers of the World* pour sa composition et sa forme. (GBR)

INDUSTRY

INDUSTRIES

INDUSTRIE

INDUSTRIES

PHOTOGRAPHER:
JIM SIMS
CLIENT:
RMI
ART DIRECTOR:
STEVEN SESSIONS
DESIGNER:
STEVEN SESSIONS
AGENCY:
STEVEN SESSIONS, INC.
■ 268-271

■ 268-271 Photographs from a brochure for RMI, an investment advisory firm, providing loans for real estate projects. The only comment to the photographs reads: "RMI. Growth and security, in expert hands." (USA)

■ 268-271 Aufnahmen aus einer Firmenbroschüre für RMI, ein Finanzierungsunternehmen für das Baugewerbe. Der einzige Kommentar zu den Aufnahmen lautet: «RMI. Wachstum und Sicherheit, in den Händen von Experten.». (USA)

■ 268-271 Photos illustrant une brochure de RMI, société de financement pour les entreprises du bâtiment. Le seul commentaire accompagnant ces illustrations, c'est «RMI. Croissance et sécurité confiées aux spécialistes.» (USA)

PHOTOGRAPHER:
FLAVIO BONETTI
CLIENT:
L'UOMO
PUBLISHER:
CONDÉ NAST S.P.A.
ART DIRECTOR:
ARMANDO CHITOLINA
DESIGNER:
FLAVIO BONETTI
■ 272

PHOTOGRAPHER:
CLAUS DIETER GEISSLER
CLIENT:
FUJI PHOTO FILM (EUROPE)
ART DIRECTOR:
GERD WOLF
AGENCY:
LINTAS HAMBURG
■ 273

PHOTOGRAPHER:
CLAUS DIETER GEISSLER
CLIENT:
CLAUS DIETER GEISSLER
■ 274

■ 272 A United States Army 9-caliber Beretta is the subject of this photograph from a feature in *L'Uomo*. (ITA)

■ 273 Photograph from an ad campaign targeted at professional photographers, for *Fuji Photo Film (Europe)*. (GER)

■ 274 Cologne photographer Claus Dieter Geissler took this shot which he uses as self-promotion. (GER)

■ 272 Eine Beretta Kaliber 9 der U.S. Army ist Gegenstand dieser Aufnahme aus einem Beitrag in *L'Uomo*. (ITA)

■ 273 Aufnahme aus einer an Berufsphotographen gerichteten Werbekampagne für *Fuji Photo Film (Europe)*. (GER)

■ 274 Als Eigenwerbung des Kölner Photographen Claus Dieter Geissler verwendete Aufnahme. (GER)

■ 272 Un Beretta 9 mm utilisé par l'armée américaine est le sujet de cette photo illustrant un article de *L'Uomo*. (ITA)

■ 273 Campagne publicitaire visant les professionnels, pour le compte de *Fuji Photo Film (Europe)*. (GER)

■ 274 Photo que le photographe Claus Dieter Geissler de Cologne utilise pour sa publicité personnelle. (GER)

■ 275 A shot used on the cover of a promotional brochure for the paper producers *Mead.* (USA)

■ 276, 277 Double-spread photographs of two *Bugatti* models, an automobile marque that was a legend in its own time. 1500 of these "sculptures in movement" still exist today – in perfect running order – in museums and auto clubs. From the German edition of the Italian magazine FMR *(Franco Maria Ricci).* (GER)

■ 275 Für den Umschlag einer Werbebroschüre des Papierherstellers *Mead* verwendete Aufnahme. (USA)

■ 276, 277 Doppelseitige Aufnahmen von zwei *Bugatti*-Modellen, eine Automarke, die zur Legende einer Epoche wurde. 1500 dieser «Skulpturen in Bewegung» stehen heute noch fahrbereit in Museen und in den Clublokalen der Liebhaber. Aus der deutschen Ausgabe der italienischen Zeitschrift FMR *(Franco Maria Ricci).* (GER)

■ 275 Photo utilisée pour la couverture d'une brochure publicitaire du papetier *Mead.* (USA)

■ 276, 277 Photos double page de deux modèles *Bugatti,* une marque de voiture devenue légendaire. 1500 de ces «sculptures en mouvement» sont encore en état de marche dans les musées de l'automobile et dans les clubs automobiles privés. Extrait de l'édition allemande du magazine italien FMR *(Franco Maria Ricci).* (GER)

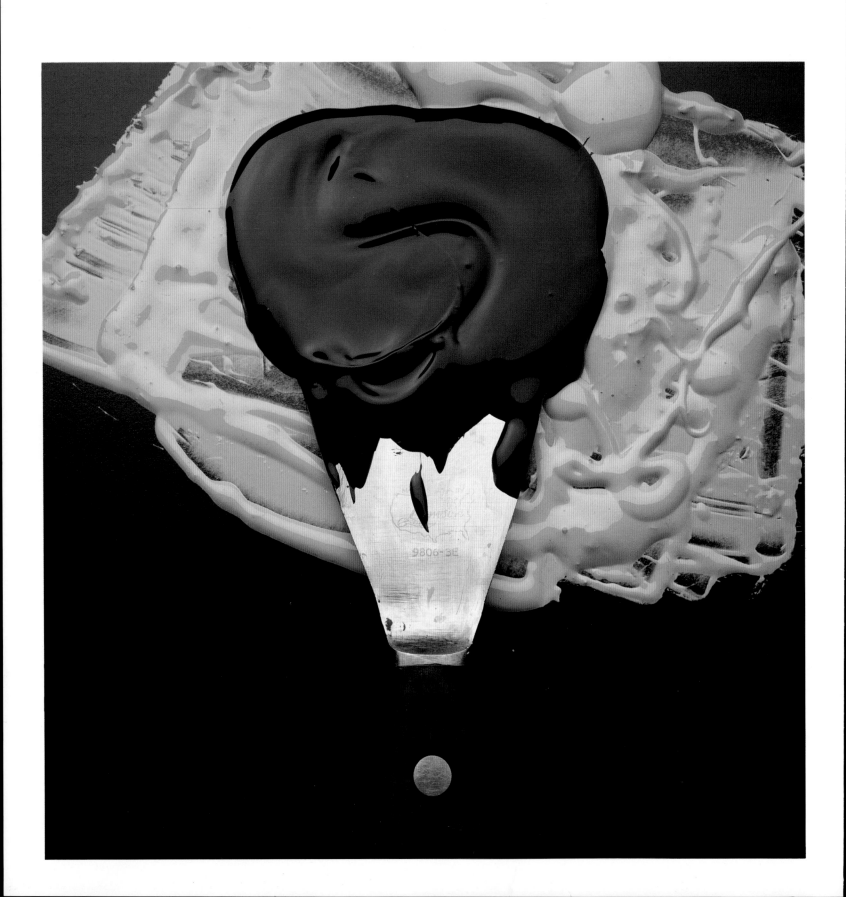

PHOTOGRAPHER:
Terry Heffernan
CLIENT:
Mead Paper
ART DIRECTOR:
John Van Dyke
DESIGNER:
John Van Dyke
AGENCY:
John Van Dyke Design
◀■ 275

PHOTOGRAPHER:
Massimo Listri
PUBLISHER:
Magazinpresse Verlag
ART DIRECTOR:
Franco Maria Ricci
▶■ 276, 277

PHOTOGRAPHER:
JIMMY WILLIAMS
CLIENT:
FIRST WACHOVIA BANK
ART DIRECTOR:
RON MORGAN
AGENCY:
LONG, HAYMES & CARR
■ 278

PHOTOGRAPHER:
ALAIN ERNOULT
CLIENT:
DASSAULT/PARIS MATCH
ART DIRECTOR:
ALAIN ERNOULT
AGENCY:
ERNOULT FEATURES
■ 279

■ 278 "The Accuracy Factor" is the title of this photograph for a poster of the First Wachovia Bank. (USA)

■ 279 Shot of the fighter plane *Rafale* by the French airplane manufacturer *Dassault.* (FRA)

■ 280 Photograph of a prototype car by the *Ford Motor Company.* The name of this model is "ASC Vision". (USA)

■ 278 »Der Genauigkeitsfaktor« ist der Titel dieser Aufnahme für ein Plakat der First Wachovia Bank. (USA)

■ 279 Photographie des Jagdbombers *Rafale* des französischen Flugzeugherstellers *Dassault.* (FRA)

■ 280 »ASC Vision« – Prototyp des amerikanischen Automobilherstellers *Ford Motor Company.* (USA)

■ 278 »Le Facteur de précision«, telle est la légende de cette photo illustrant une affiche de la First Wachovia Bank. (USA)

■ 279 Vue de l'avion de chasse *Rafale,* prototype de l'avionneur français *Dassault.* (FRA)

■ 280 Photo d'un prototype de la *Ford Motor Company* baptisé «ASC Vision». (USA)

PHOTOGRAPHER:
ANTHONY ARCIERO
CLIENT:
FORD MOTOR CO.
ART DIRECTOR:
HEIDI W. ZUCCO
DESIGNER:
HEIDI W. ZUCCO
AGENCY:
YOUNG & RUBICAM DETROIT
■ 280

PHOTOGRAPHER:
STEVE MCMAHON
CLIENT:
STEVE MCMAHON
ART DIRECTOR:
STEVE MCMAHON
■ 281

PHOTOGRAPHER:
DIETMAR HENNEKA
CLIENT:
*MERCEDES-BENZ OF
NORTH AMERICA, INC.*
ART DIRECTOR:
GUNTHER MAIER
DESIGNER:
GUNTHER MAIER
AGENCY:
MCCAFFREY & MCCALL, INC.
■ 282

■ 281 Photograph of a Porsche taken by Steve McMahon and used by him as self-promotion. (USA)

■ 282 Full-page photograph from an ad for *Mercedes-Benz*, USA. The S Class models shown here were made in 1955, 1963, 1972 and 1987 (up front). (USA)

■ 283 This photograph appeared on the back cover of a *Porsche* advertising brochure. (GER)

■ 281 Als Eigenwerbung des Photographen Steve McMahon verwendete Aufnahme eines Porsche. (USA)

■ 282 Ganzseitige Aufnahme aus einer Anzeige für *Mercedes-Benz*, USA. Diese Modelle der S-Klasse stammen aus den Jahren 1955, 1963, 1972 und 1987 (ganz vorne). (USA)

■ 283 Für die vierte Umschlagseite einer *Porsche*-Werbebroschüre verwendete Aufnahme. (GER)

■ 281 Photo d'une Porsche utilisée par le photographe Steve McMahon pour sa promotion. (USA)

■ 282 Photo pleine page pour une annonce de *Mercedes-Benz* aux Etats-Unis. Les modèles de la classe S présentés ici sont de 1955, 1963, 1972 et 1987 (au premier plan). (USA)

■ 283 Photo utilisée pour la quatrième page de couverture d'une brochure promotionnelle *Porsche*. (GER)

PHOTOGRAPHER:
VOLKER MEISSNER
CLIENT:
DR. ING. H.C.F. PORSCHE AG
ART DIRECTOR:
ALBRECHT ADE
DESIGNER:
ALBRECHT ADE
■ 283

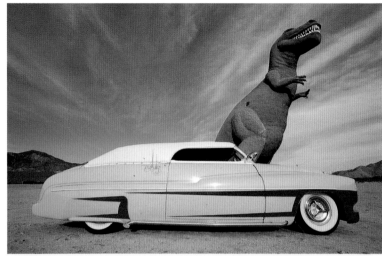

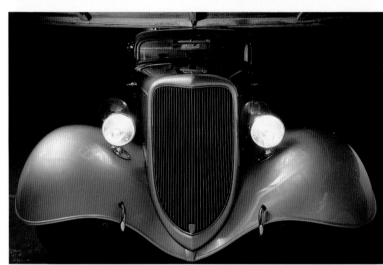

PHOTOGRAPHER:
Clint Clemens
CLIENT:
Clint Clemens
ART DIRECTOR:
Bill Clark
AGENCY:
Bozell, Jacobs, Kenyon
& Eckhardt
■ 284

PHOTOGRAPHER:
Clint Clemens
CLIENT:
S.D. Warren Paper Co.
ART DIRECTOR:
Cheryl Heller
AGENCY:
HBM/Creamer
■ 285-289

■ 284-289 Photographs of Old Timers. *284:* 1930 Rolls Royce Phantom II photographed in New Hampshire and used for self-promotional purposes; remaining shots taken in California for advertising purposes for the *S.D. Warren* Paper Company: *285, 286:* two Mercurys from 1950, *287-289:* Ford models from 1934 and 1937. (USA)

■ 290 Cover photograph from the 1987 calendar for BMW, entitled "BMW in Japan". Since the beginning of the 1980's BMW has been successful with its own company in Japan. (JPN)

■ 284-289 Old Timer - *284:* ein Rolls Royce Phantom II 1930, in New Hampshire photographiert und für Eigenwerbung verwendet; die übrigen Aufnahmen entstanden in Kalifornien und wurden für die Werbung des Papierherstellers *S.D. Warren* verwendet. *285, 286:* zwei Mercurys Baujahr 1950, *287-289:* Ford-Modelle von 1934 und 1937. (USA)

■ 290 Aufnahme aus einem Wandkalender von BMW für 1987, mit dem Titel «BMW am Beispiel Japan». Seit Anfang der 80er Jahre ist BMW erfolgreich mit einer eigenen Gesellschaft in Japan tätig. (JPN)

■ 284-289 Voitures de collection - *284:* une Rolls Royce Phantom II de 1930, photographiée dans le New Hampshire pour l'autopromotion du photographe; les 5 autres photos ont été réalisées en Californie pour une campagne du papetier *S.D. Warren. 285, 286:* deux Mercury 1950, *287-289:* modèles Ford des années 1934 et 1937. (USA)

■ 290 Photo illustrant le calendrier BMW pour 1987 intitulé «BMW au Japon». Depuis le début des années 1980, BMW développe ses activités au Japon, où l'entreprise allemande a créé une société de distribution. (JPN)

PHOTOGRAPHER:
THOMAS LÜTTGE
CLIENT:
BMW AG
ART DIRECTOR:
WALTER SCHWAIGER
DESIGNER:
WALTER SCHWAIGER
AGENCY:
BÜRO SCHWAIGER
■ 290

PHOTOGRAPHER:
Roy D. Query
PUBLISHER:
CBS Inc.
ART DIRECTOR:
Michael Pardo
DESIGNER:
Michael Pardo
■ 291

■ 291 "Corvette, an American Legend" is the title of the publication by *Automobile Quarterly* from which this photograph is taken. (USA)

■ 292 From a calendar for *Sinar* objectives, with shots of cars by various renowned photographers. (SWI)

■ 291 «Corvette, eine amerikanische Legende» ist der Titel der Publikation von *Automobile Quarterly*, aus der diese Aufnahme stammt. (USA)

■ 292 Aus einem Kalender für *Sinar*-Objektive mit Autoaufnahmen verschiedener bekannter Photographen. (SWI)

■ 291 «Corvette, une légende américaine» – c'est ainsi que s'intitule la publication d'*Automobile Quarterly* d'où est tirée cette photo. (USA)

■ 292 Calendrier illustré de photos de voitures par divers photographes de renom, pour les objectifs *Sinar*. (SWI)

PHOTOGRAPHER:
MANFRED RIEKER
CLIENT:
SINAR AG
ART DIRECTOR:
PETER G. ULMER
DESIGNER:
PETER G. ULMER
AGENCY:
ATELIER P.G. ULMER
■ 292

PHOTOGRAPHER:
JOHN CLARIDGE
■ 293

■ 293 "Yellow Truck" is the title of this personal study by London photographer John Claridge. (GBR)

■ 293 «Yellow Truck» (Gelber Lastwagen) - Persönliche Studie des Londoner Photographen John Claridge. (GBR)

■ 293 «Yellow Truck» (Camion jaune) - étude personnelle du photographe londonien John Claridge. (GBR)

SPORTS

SPORT

SPORT

PHOTOGRAPHER:
LACI PERÉNYI
PUBLISHER:
GRUNER + JAHR AG & CO.
ART DIRECTOR:
FRANZ EPPING
■ 294

PHOTOGRAPHER:
*Hans Jürgen Burkard/
Bilderberg*
PUBLISHER:
Gruner + Jahr AG & Co.
ART DIRECTOR:
Franz Epping
■ 295

■ 294 Double-spread photograph from an article in *Sports* on the 1987 World Cup in Rome. Shown is Carl Lewis after a vault of 8,67 meters. (GER)

■ 295 Photograph of the East German swimmer Frank Hoffmeister (since defected to the West), from an article in the magazine *Sports* devoted to this athlete. (GER)

■ 294 Doppelseitige Aufnahme aus einem Beitrag in *Sports* über die Weltmeisterschaft '87 in Rom. Hier Carl Lewis nach einem Sprung von 8,67 Metern. (GER)

■ 295 Aufnahme des inzwischen in die Bundesrepublik geflüchteten DDR-Schwimmers Frank Hoffmeister, aus einem Beitrag in der Zeitschrift *Sports*. (GER)

■ 294 Photo double page illustrant un article de *Sports* où il est question des championnats du monde 1987 à Rome. On voit ici Carl Lewis après son saut de 8,67 m. (GER)

■ 295 Photo de l'as est-allemand de la natation Frank Hoffmeister, entre-temps réfugié en RFA, dans un article que le magazine *Sports* consacre à ce sportif. (GER)

PHOTOGRAPHER:
JOE BARABAN
CLIENT:
JOE BARABAN PHOTOGRAPHY, INC.
DESIGNER:
JOHN WEAVER
AGENCY:
GLUTH/WEAVER
■ 296

■ 296 Thoroughbred horses and riding are the subject of this photograph by Joe Baraban. From his portfolio entitled "Shoot at Joe's". (USA)

■ 297 Photograph of a sailing regatta in Sweden's archipelago from an article devoted to this country in *Geo*. (GER)

■ 296 Rassepferde und der Reitsport sind Gegenstand dieser Aufnahme des Photographen Joe Baraban. Aus seinem Portfolio «Shoot at Joe's». (USA)

■ 297 Aufnahme einer Segelregatta in den Schären Schwedens, aus einem Artikel über dieses Land in *Geo*. (GER)

■ 296 Les chevaux de sang et les sports équestres sont le sujet de cette photo du photographe Joe Baraban. Prise de son portfolio «Shoot at Joe's». (USA)

■ 297 Photo d'une régate organisée entre les îlots rocheux au large des côtes suédoises, dans un article de *Geo*. (GER)

PHOTOGRAPHER:
MARC IZIKOWITZ
PUBLISHER:
GRUNER + JAHR AG & CO.
ART DIRECTOR:
ERWIN EHRET
■ 297

PHOTOGRAPHER:
DETLEF SCHUMACHER
PUBLISHER:
PHOTO DESIGN +
TECHNIK GMBH
ART DIRECTOR:
LUTZ LUTZ DESIGN
■ 298

■ 298 Double-spread photograph of a surfer, from an article in *Photo Design + Technik*. Photographer Detlef Schumacher was himself a sports teacher up to a few years ago. The photographs in this series were taken in Hawaii, the majority of them from a rubber dinghy – with such giant waves, an assignment not without risk. (SWI)

■ 299 "Texas, a University Portrait", photograph from a promotion booklet for the University of Texas. Shown are students practicing in Town Lake in a rowboat. (USA)

■ 298 Doppelseitige Aufnahme eines Surfers, aus einem Artikel in *Photo Design + Technik*. Der Photograph Detlef Schumacher war bis vor einigen Jahren noch Sportlehrer. Die Aufnahmen dieser Serie entstanden vor Hawaii, die meisten von ihnen vom Schlauchboot aus, was bei den Mammutwellen kein ungefährliches Unterfangen war. (SWI)

■ 299 Ganzseitige Aufnahme aus einer Werbepublikation der Universität von Texas. Hier eine der vielen Sportarten, unter denen die Studenten wählen können. (USA)

■ 298 Photo d'un surfeur, illustrant un article de *Photo Design + Technik*. Il y a quelques années, Detlef Schumacher était encore professeur d'éducation physique. Il a réalisé ces photos au large des îles Hawaii, la plupart depuis un canot pneumatique, ce qui n'était pas sans danger vu la puissance des vagues déferlant sur le littoral. (SWI)

■ 299 Photo double page dans une brochure publicitaire de l'Université du Texas. On y voit l'une des nombreuses disciplines sportives qui s'offrent aux étudiants. (USA)

PHOTOGRAPHER:
ARTHUR MEYERSON
CLIENT:
*THE EX-STUDENTS'
ASSOCIATION OF THE
UNIVERSITY OF TEXAS*
ART DIRECTOR:
JAMES PATRICK
DESIGNER:
DONALD PAULHUS
■ 299

PHOTOGRAPHER:
CONNY J. WINTER
CLIENT:
WINTER/BERTSCH/DOMBERGER
ART DIRECTOR:
CONNY J. WINTER
DESIGNER:
CONNY J. WINTER
■ 300-303

■ 300-303 Photographs from a calendar entitled "Sport 87", in which different sports are visualized. Various companies placed their proprietary products at disposal for the photographs. (GER)

■ 300-303 Aufnahmen aus einem Wandkalender mit dem Titel «Sport 87», in dem verschiedene Sportarten visualisiert werden. Verschiedene Markenfirmen stellten ihre Produkte für die Aufnahmen zur Verfügung. (GER)

■ 300-303 Photos extraites d'un calendrier mural publié sous le titre de «Sport 87». On y visualise diverses disciplines en mettant en scène les équipements prêtés par les fabricants de produits de marque. (GER)

JOURNALISM

JOURNALISME

JOURNALISMUS

JOURNALISM

JOURNALISME

PHOTOGRAPHER:
SEBASTIÃO SALGADO/
MAGNUM
PUBLISHER:
PUBLICATION FILIPACCHI
ART DIRECTOR:
ERIC COLMET DAAGE
■ 304–308

■ 304–308 Shots from a photo essay, the first part of a pro-ject by photographer Sebastião Salgado, which is to be con-tinued over several years. The title: "Archeology of the Industrial Age – Productive Man at the Threshold of the 21st Century". The photographs were taken in a crater of the Serra Pelada, Brazil. Until recently there were forests and a mountain in this region – now there is a frantic gold rush. From an article in *Photo*. (FRA)

■ 304–308 Aus einer Photoreportage, einem Projekt des Photographen Sebastião Salgado, das sich noch über meh-rere Jahre hinziehen wird. Der Titel: «Archäologie des indu-striellen Zeitalters: der arbeitende Mensch an der Schwelle zum 21. Jahrhundert.» Die Aufnahmen entstanden in einem Krater in der Serra Pelada, Brasilien. Hier gab es bis vor kur-zem noch Wald und einen Berg – jetzt wird fieberhaft nach Gold gesucht. Aus einem Beitrag in *Photo*. (FRA)

■ 304–308 Photos faisant partie d'un reportage conçu par le photographe Sebastião Salgado comme le premier volet d'un projet qui mettra encore de longues années à se réali-ser. Le titre: «Archéologie de l'époque industrielle: l'homme productif à l'aube du XXIe siècle.» Ces photos ont été prises dans un cratère de la Serra Pelada, au Brésil. Là où il y avait des forêts, une montagne, la nature est bouleversée par les chercheurs d'or. Article paru dans *Photo*. (FRA)

PHOTOGRAPHER:
EMMET W. FRANCOIS
PUBLISHER:
WELCOME ENTERPRISES, INC.
ART DIRECTOR:
NAI Y. CHANG
DESIGNER:
JOHN ALEXANDER
AGENCY:
WELCOME ENTERPRISES, INC.
■ 309

PHOTOGRAPHER:
FRANCO ZECCHIN
PUBLISHER:
NEW YORK TIMES MAGAZINE
◄■ 311, 312

PHOTOGRAPHER:
FRANCESCO CITO
PUBLISHER:
GRUNER + JAHR AG & CO.
ART DIRECTOR:
FRANZ EPPING
■ 313

■ 311, 312 Scenes of Palermo. In the house of poor people in the Kalsa area, and the wife and daughters of the murdered Benedetto Grado, at the scene of the crime. They were still mourning their son murdered six months earlier. From the *New York Times Magazine*. (USA)

■ 313 Photograph from the magazine *Sports*, taken on the day Naples won the Italian soccer championship. It was a sensation since the title, with one previous exception, has always gone to soccer clubs of the north. (ITA)

■ 311, 312 Bilder aus Palermo: im Hause von armen Leuten im Kalsa-Viertel und Frau und Töchter des ermordeten Benedetto Grado am Ort des Verbrechens. Sie trauern bereits um den 6 Monate vorher getöteten Sohn. Aus *New York Times Magazine*. (USA)

■ 313 Doppelseitige Aufnahme aus der Zeitschrift *Sports:* Der Tag, an dem Neapel italienischer Fussballmeister wurde – eine Sensation, denn seit Bestehen der Liga ging der Titel, mit einer Ausnahme, an die Clubs aus dem Norden. (ITA)

■ 311, 312 Images de Palerme: dans une famille pauvre du quartier de Kalsa; la veuve et les filles de Benedetto Grado lâchement assassiné, sur les lieux du crime, éplorées après le meurtre du fils 6 mois plus tôt. Dans *New York Times Magazine*. (USA)

■ 313 Photo double page publiée dans le magazine *Sports:* le jour où le FC de Naples remporta le championnat d'Italie – une victoire qui fit sensation, les clubs du Nord de la Ligue s'étant toujours attribué le titre, à une exception près. (ITA)

PHOTOGRAPHER:
DENNIS CARLYLE DARLING
PUBLISHER:
DORSODURO PRESS
ART DIRECTOR:
DENNIS CARLYLE DARLING
DESIGNER:
DENNIS CARLYLE DARLING
■ 314

PHOTOGRAPHER:
SEBASTIÃO SALGADO/
MAGNUM
■ 315

■ 314 Photograph from the book "Desperate Pleasures" a monography by Dennis Carlyle Darling. This picture was taken in Guanajuato, Mexico. (USA)

■ 315 Shot taken in Ecuador by photojournalist Sebastião Salgado. This photograph was used for the invitations to his exhibitions "The Other America" and "Sahel, People in Need". (FRA)

■ 314 Aufnahme aus dem Buch «Desperate Pleasures», einer Monographie von Dennis Carlyle Darling. Diese Photographie entstand in Guanajuato, Mexiko. (USA)

■ 315 In Ecuador entstandene Aufnahme des Photojournalisten Sebastião Salgado, die als Einladungskarte für seine Ausstellungen «Das andere Amerika» und «Sahel, Menschen in Not» verwendet wurde. (FRA)

■ 314 Photo extraite de l'ouvrage «Desperate Pleasures», une monographie de Dennis Carlyle Darling. Vue réalisée à Guanajuato, au Mexique. (USA)

■ 315 Photo réalisée par le reporter photo Sebastião Salgado, utilisée pour l'invitation à ses deux expositions «Autres Amériques» et «Sahel, l'homme en détresse» organisées à Lausanne. (FRA)

PHOTOGRAPHER:
KARL GRIMES
PUBLISHER:
THE ARTS COUNCIL OF IRELAND
ART DIRECTOR:
KARL GRIMES
AGENCY:
*KARL GRIMES STUDIO/
ONE-OFF PRODUCTIONS*
■ 319

■ 319 Photograph for a book and an exhibition about life in the Irish Army. (IRL)

■ 320 From a book (*Econ* press) by photographer Dieter Blum, entitled *Auslöser* ("Trigger"). This war memorial outside the church of St. Dionysus reads: "Fearless and Faithful". In spray are the words: "and dead!". (GER)

■ 319 Aufnahme für ein Buch und eine Ausstellung über das Leben in der irischen Armee. (IRL)

■ 320 Doppelseitige Aufnahme aus einem bei *Econ* erschienenen Buch des Photographen Dieter Blum mit dem Titel *Auslöser*. Dieses Kriegsdenkmal befindet sich an der Esslinger Stadtkirche St. Dionys. (GER)

■ 319 Photo pour un livre et une exposition consacrés à la vie dans l'armée irlandaise. (IRL)

■ 320 Photo illustrant un album du photographe Dieter Blum paru aux Editions *Econ* sous le titre de *Auslöser* (Déclencheur). Monument aux morts «intrépides et fidèles» – «et bien morts», a ajouté un sprayeur anonyme. (GER)

PHOTOGRAPHER:
DIETER BLUM
PUBLISHER:
ECON VERLAG GMBH
ART DIRECTOR:
KURT WEIDEMANN
DESIGNER:
KURT WEIDEMANN
STUDIO:
DIETER BLUM
■ 320

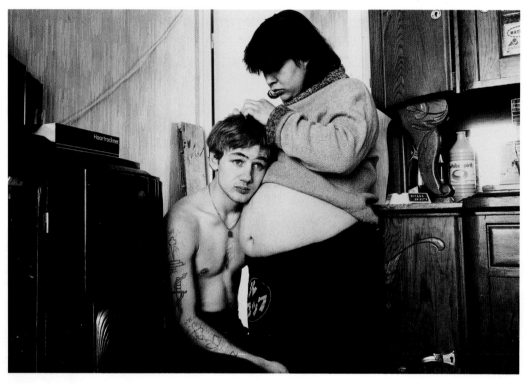 

PHOTOGRAPHER:
SERGE SIBERT
PUBLISHER:
PUBLICATION FILIPACCHI
ART DIRECTOR:
ERIC COLMET DAAGE
■ 321, 322

■ 321, 322 Shots taken by photo-journalist Serge Sibert, published under the title "Lost Children" in the magazine *Photo.* Shown are the photographs of a pregnant 17-year-old girl and a young father of 18. (FRA)

■ 323 This photo of a woman misused as a tray was taken in a Japanese sushi restaurant, which specializes in presenting its food in this manner. Double spread from the photo book *Dieter Blum – Auslöser* («Trigger»), *Econ* press. (GER)

■ 321, 322 Aufnahmen des Photojournalisten Serge Sibert, die unter dem Titel «Verlorene Kinder» in der Zeitschrift *Photo* erschienen: Eine schwangere Jugendliche und ein 18jähriger Vater. (FRA)

■ 323 Eine als Tablett missbrauchte Frau in einem Sushi-Restaurant, das sich auf die Darbietung seiner Speisen auf diese Art spezialisiert hat. Doppelseite aus dem Photoband *Dieter Blum – Auslöser, Econ*-Verlag. (GER)

■ 321, 322 Photos extraites d'un reportage de Serge Sibert paru dans le magazine *Photo* sous le titre d'«Enfants perdus» - en l'occurrence, une adolescente enceinte de 17 ans et un jeune père de 18 ans. (FRA)

■ 323 Une femme utilisée comme plateau porte-plats dans un restaurant Sushi qui «innove» de cette manière dans la présentation de ses plats. Double page de l'album *Dieter Blum – Auslöser* (Déclencheur), aux Ed. *Econ*. (GER)

PHOTOGRAPHER:
DIETER BLUM
PUBLISHER:
ECON VERLAG GMBH
ART DIRECTOR:
KURT WEIDEMANN
DESIGNER:
KURT WEIDEMANN
STUDIO:
DIETER BLUM
■ 323

■ 324 "Street Vendor of Flowers", Hanoi, Vietnam. One of a series of photographs taken in Vietnam by photo journalist Geoffrey Clifford. (USA)

■ 325-328 "After Midnight". Examples of a photo essay about American youth. (USA)

■ 324 Blumenverkäuferin, Hanoi, Vietnam. Aus einer Serie von Aufnahmen des Photographen Geoffrey Clifford, die in Vietnam entstanden. (USA)

■ 325-328 Beispiele aus einer Photoserie über die amerikanische Jugend mit dem Titel «Nach Mitternacht». (USA)

■ 324 Vendeuse de fleurs dans une rue de Hanoi, au Viêtnam. Photo réalisée par le reporter Geoffrey Clifford au cours d'une enquête au Viêt-nam. (USA)

■ 325-328 Exemples d'un reportage photo sur la jeunesse américaine paru sous le titre d'«Après minuit». (USA)

PHOTOGRAPHER:
GEOFFREY CLIFFORD/
WHEELER PICTURES
PUBLISHER:
GRANDS REPORTAGES
ART DIRECTOR:
BRUM BARBIER
■ 324

PHOTOGRAPHER:
THOMAS BRUMMETT
PUBLISHER:
THOMAS BRUMMETT
ART DIRECTOR:
THOMAS BRUMMETT
■ 325-328

PHOTOGRAPHER:
MICHAEL LANGE/VISUM
PUBLISHER:
GRUNER + JAHR AG & CO.
ART DIRECTOR:
ERWIN EHRET
■ 329

■ 329 Photograph from an article in *Geo* relating to the hard times experienced by farmers in the United States. Shown here is a farmer's house in Iowa being transported, subsequent to its auction. (GER)

■ 329 Aufnahme aus einem Artikel in *Geo,* in dem es um die schlechte Lage der Bauern in den Vereinigten Staaten geht. Hier wird nach einer Versteigerung das Haus eines Bauern in Iowa abtransportiert. (GER)

■ 329 Photo pour un article du magazine *Geo* où il est question du sort peu enviable des agriculteurs américains. On voit ici le déménagement de la maison d'un fermier au terme d'une vente de ses biens aux enchères. (GER)

STILL LIFE

NATURE MORTE

STILLEBEN

PHOTOGRAPHER:
TERRY HEFFERNAN
CLIENT:
POTLATCH CORP.
DESIGNER:
ERIC MADSEN/KEVIN KUESTER
AGENCY:
MADSEN & KUESTER, INC.
■ 330-332

■ 330-332 These photographs are taken from a brochure for *Karma* paper by *Potlatch*. The subjects chosen are the symbols of various old and new cultures. Shown are requisites from the Hopi Indian tribe used for nine religious ceremonies every year; the typical eagle masks worn by Shamans of the Tlingit Indians, and the simple hat worn by members of the Amish sect. (USA)

■ 330-332 Symbole verschiedener Kulturen alter und neuerer Zeit sind Gegenstand dieser Aufnahmen aus einer Broschüre für *Karma*-Papier von *Potlatch*. Hier Requisiten, die vom Hopi-Stamm alljährlich für neun religiöse Zeremonien verwendet werden; die typischen Adlermasken der Schamanen des Tlingit-Stammes und der schlichte Hut der Angehörigen der Amish-Sekte. (USA)

■ 330-332 Les symboles de plusieurs civilisations anciennes et modernes sont le sujet de ces illustrations d'une brochure *Potlatch* consacrée au papier *Karma:* accessoires que les Indiens Hopis utilisent pour neuf cérémonies religieuses annuelles; masques d'aigle tels qu'en portent les chamans de la tribu Tlingit; couvre-chef des membres de la secte des Amish, remarquable de simplicité. (USA)

■ 333 "British Virgin Islands" - photograph from a diary used as joint promotion for photographer Tim Bieber and the printers *Burch*. (USA)

■ 334-337 Photographer Loni Liebermann plays with filters and lighting intervals, aiming at the many possibilities to disperse the color spectrum and to achieve complementary shading tones. (GER)

■ 333 «British Virgin Islands», Aufnahme aus einer Agenda, die als Gemeinschaftswerbung für den Photographen Tim Bieber und die Druckerei *Burch* dient. (USA)

■ 334-337 Die Photographin Loni Liebermann spielt mit Filtern, Belichtungsintervallen, mit den vielen Möglichkeiten, das Farbspektrum aufzulösen und komplementäre Schattenfarben zu erzielen. (GER)

■ 333 «Les Îles Vierges britanniques»: photo tirée d'un agenda utilisé pour la publicité collective du photographe Tim Bieber et de l'imprimerie *Burch*. (USA)

■ 334-337 La photographe Loni Liebermann est passée experte dans l'art de combiner les filtres, les intervalles d'exposition, les couleurs du spectre de manière à obtenir des couleurs complémentaires ombrées. (GER)

PHOTOGRAPHER:
TIM BIEBER
CLIENT:
TIM BIEBER PHOTOGRAPHY
DESIGNER:
STEVE LISKA
■ 333

PHOTOGRAPHER:
LONI LIEBERMANN
■ 334-337

PHOTOGRAPHER:
JEAN-BLAISE HALL
CLIENT:
BLUE RIBBON SUPPLY
ART DIRECTOR:
STEVE GILBERT
AGENCY:
SGA
■ 338-340

PHOTOGRAPHER:
LOU GOODMAN
CLIENT:
MARCOVICI DESIGNS
ART DIRECTOR:
BRENT MARMO/LIZ ROTTER
DESIGNER:
LIZ ROTTER
AGENCY:
THE BROWNSTONE GROUP, INC.
►■ 341, 342

■ 338-340 Photographs from the brochure for *Blue Ribbon Supply*, a company specialized in hotel supply. (USA)

■ 341, 342 Photographs from a catalog for *Marcovici Designs*, an importer of European quality products. (USA)

■ 338-340 Beispiele der Aufnahmen aus einer Broschüre für *Blue Ribbon Supply*, eine Firma für Hotelzubehör. (USA)

■ 341, 342 Aus einem Katalog für *Marcovici Designs*, einen Importeur europäischer Qualitäts-Produkte. (USA)

■ 338-340 Photos illustrant une brochure de *Blue Ribbon Supply*, une maison d'equipements hôteliers. (USA)

■ 341, 342 Photos d'un catalogue de *Marcovici Designs*, qui importe des produits de qualité européens. (USA)

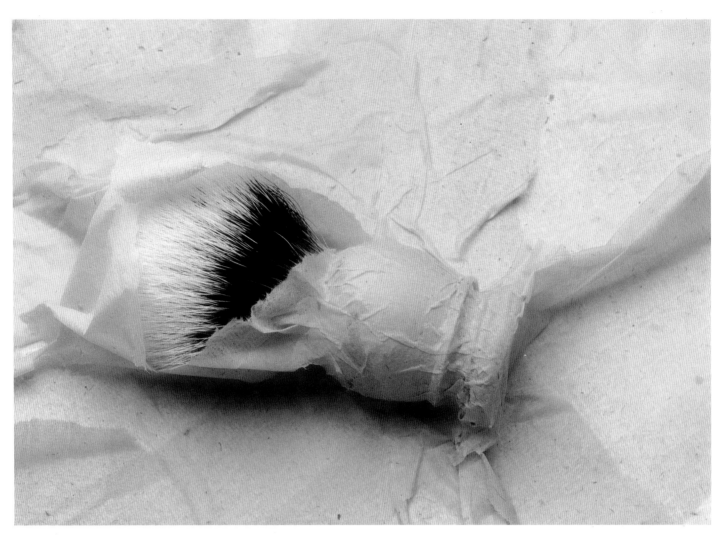

PHOTOGRAPHER:
STUART MCINTYRE
CLIENT:
HI TECH
ART DIRECTOR:
ULLA HEEGAARD
■ 343

PHOTOGRAPHER:
DENNIS BLACHUT
CLIENT:
DENNIS BLACHUT
ART DIRECTOR:
DENNIS BLACHUT
►■ 344

■ 343 Shot by photographer Stuart McIntyre, displaying one of his specialties, still life. (DEN)

■ 344 Self-promotion for American photographer Dennis Blachut. (USA)

■ 343 Aufnahme des Photographen Stuart McIntyre, der sich u.a. auf Stilleben spezialisiert hat. (DEN)

■ 344 Eigenwerbung des amerikanischen Photographen Dennis Blachut. (USA)

■ 343 Création du photographe Stuart McIntyre, dont l'une des spécialités est la nature morte. (DEN)

■ 344 Autopromotion du photographe americain Dennis Blachut. (USA)

PHOTOGRAPHER:
YURI DOJC
CLIENT:
YURI DOJC
DESIGNER:
LES HOLLAWAY
■ 345

PHOTOGRAPHER:
BARRY MEEKUMS
CLIENT:
AGIO SIGARENFABRIEKEN N.V.
ART DIRECTOR:
PIM VAN DER MEER
DESIGNER:
PIM VAN DER MEER
AGENCY:
FHV/BBDO
► ■ 346, 347

■ 345 As self promotion, a shot taken by photographer Yuri Dojc, Toronto. (CAN)

■ 346, 347 Still life with cigars - photographs from an advertising campaign for Agio Sigarenfabrieken N.V., Netherlands. (NLD)

■ 345 Als Eigenwerbung verwendete Aufnahme des kanadischen Photographen Yuri Dojc. (CAN)

■ 346, 347 Stilleben mit Zigarren - Aufnahmen aus einer Werbekampagne der Firma Agio Sigarenfabrieken N.V., Holland. (NLD)

■ 345 Photo que le photographe Yuri Dojc de Toronto utilise pour sa promotion. (CAN)

■ 346, 347 Nature morte avec cigares - photos pour une campagne publicitaire pour l'entreprise Agio Sigarenfabrieken N.V., Pays-Bas. (NLD)

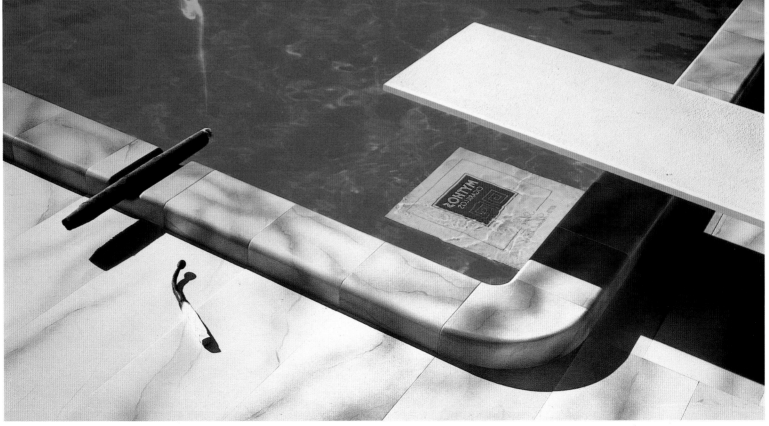

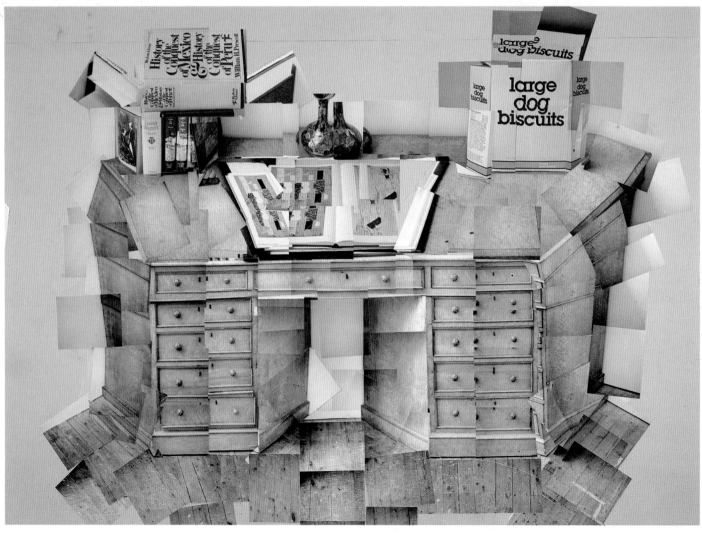

ARTIST/PHOTOGRAPHER:
DAVID HOCKNEY
SUBJECT PHOTOGRAPHY:
MARK FARRINGTON
RICHARD SCHMIDT
STEVEN SLOMAN
CLIENT:
VOGUE PARIS
PUBLISHER:
CONDÉ NAST S.A.
ART DIRECTOR:
PAUL WAGNER
■ 348-352

■ 348-352 Photographs from a special chapter in the French edition of *Vogue* entitled *"Vogue* by David Hockney". The pictures and thoughts are on time, space, illusion, seeing, drawing, color, surface, collage, printing, perception, suggestion, perspective, photography, and magazines. The previous double spread was the closing spread of the feature. Shown here from l. to r.: scene from a series about the different times of day in Los Angeles; "a typical Hollywood scene"; "Jardins du Luxembourg"; thoughts on the inversion of perspective. (FRA)

■ 348-352 Aus einem speziellen Kapitel in der französischen Ausgabe der *Vogue* mit dem Titel «*Vogue* par David Hockney»: Gedanken und Bilder über Zeit, Raum, Illusion, Sehen, Zeichnen, Farbe, Oberfläche, Collage, Druck, Wahrnehmung, Vorstellung, Perspektive, Photographie und Zeitschriften. Vorangehende Doppelseite: die abschliessende Doppelseite des Beitrags. Auf dieser Doppelseite v.l.n.r.: Bild aus einer Reihe über verschiedene Tageszeiten in Los Angeles; eine typische Hollywood-Szene; Jardins du Luxembourg; Gedanken über die Umkehrung der Perspektive. (FRA)

■ 348-352 D'un chapitre spécial de l'édition française de *Vogue* intitulé «*Vogue* par David Hockney». On y traite par le texte et par l'image toute une série de sujets: le temps, l'espace, l'illusion, le regard, le dessin, la couleur, la surface, le collage, la gravure, la perception, la suggestion, la perspective, la photographie et les magazines. Double page précédente: la double page qui clôt l'article avec, de g. à dr.: d'une série sur les diverses heures du jour à Los Angeles; scène hollywoodienne type; jardins du Luxembourg; réflexions sur l'inversion de la perspective. (FRA)

PHOTOGRAPHER:
GERHARD VORMWALD
CLIENT:
GERHARD VORMWALD
ART DIRECTOR:
GERHARD VORMWALD
◄■ 353

PHOTOGRAPHER:
MICHAEL GEIGER
■ 354

■ 353 A shot typical for photographer Gerhard Vormwald, from *Portfolio Photographie*. (SWI)

■ 353 Eine für den Photographen Gerhard Vormwald typische Aufnahme, aus *Portfolio Photographie*. (SWI)

■ 353 Photo typique du style du photographe Gerhard Vormwald publiée dans *Portfolio Photographie*. (SWI)

■ 354 Self-promotional shot by photographer Michael Geiger of New York. (USA)

■ 354 Als Eigenwerbung verwendete Aufnahme des Photographen Michael Geiger, New York. (USA)

■ 354 Image du photographe Michael Geiger de New York, qu'il utilise pour sa promotion. (USA)

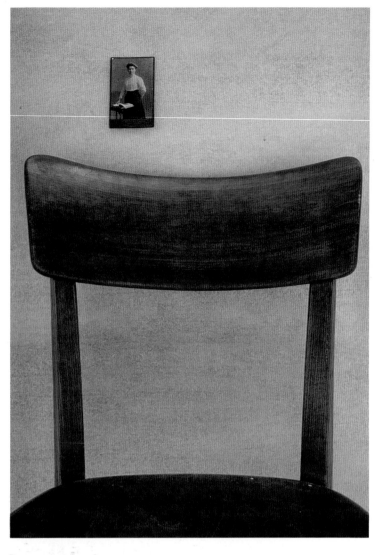

PHOTOGRAPHER:
Urs Grunder
PUBLISHER:
Verlag Photographie AG
ART DIRECTOR:
Peter Wassermann
■ 355

PHOTOGRAPHER:
David Stewart
CLIENT:
David Stewart
ART DIRECTOR:
David Stewart
■ 356

PHOTOGRAPHER:
Michael Geiger
► ■ 357

■ 355 Example of one of the "Grandmother Series" of photographs all relating to the transitoriness of life. Taken from *Portfolio Photographie*. (SWI)

■ 356 Personal study by photographer David Stewart with the title "Things". (GBR)

■ 357 "Konstruction, à la redoutée" is the title of this shot by New Yorker photographer Michael Geiger. (USA)

■ 355 Beispiel der zu einer «Grossmutter-Serie» gehörenden Aufnahmen, die sich mit der Vergänglichkeit des Lebens befassen. Aus *Portfolio Photographie*. (SWI)

■ 356 Persönliche Studie des Photographen David Stewart mit dem Titel «Dinge». (GBR)

■ 357 «Konstruction, à la redoutée» nennt der New Yorker Photograph Michael Geiger diese Aufnahme. (USA)

■ 355 Exemple des photos de la «série des grands-mères» sur le thème du caractère éphémère de la vie, que l'on trouve reproduites dans *Portfolio Photographie*. (SWI)

■ 356 Etude personnelle du photographe David Steward intitulée «Choses». (GBR)

■ 357 «Konstruction, à la redoutée» – c'est ainsi que le photographe Michael Geiger intitule sa création. (USA)

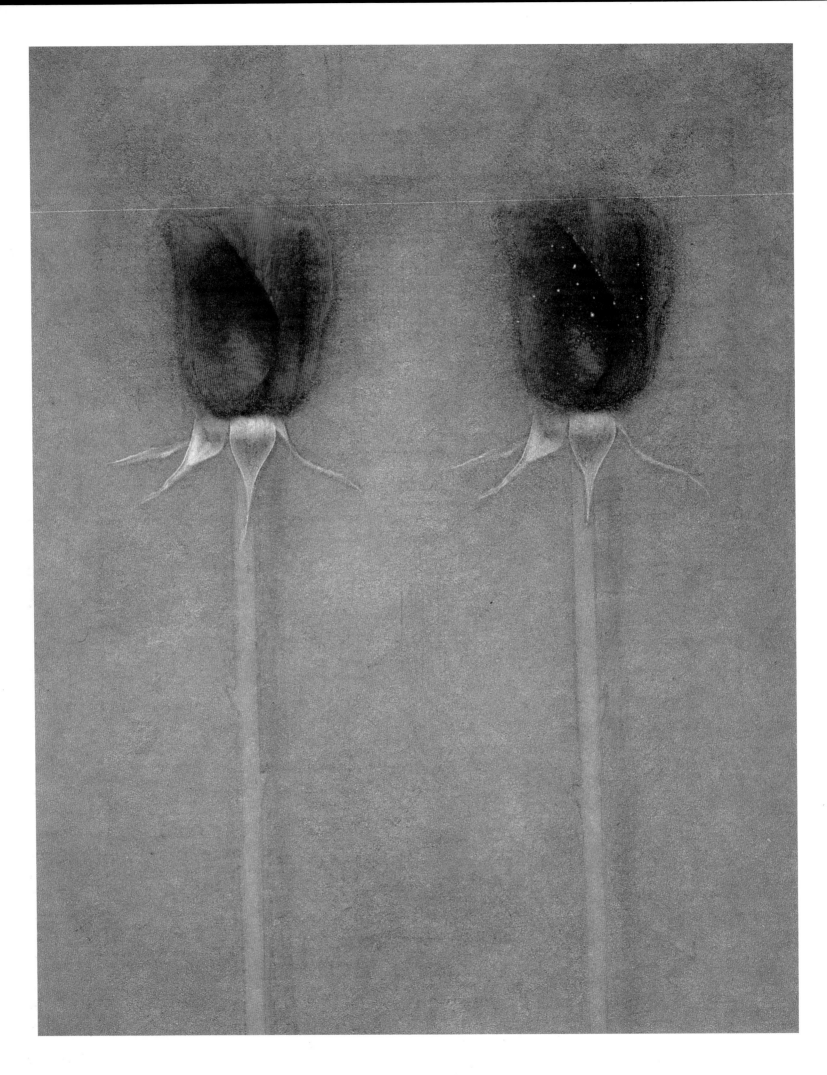

■ 358 "Two Roses" – a self-promotional shot taken by photographer Dave Holt of Los Angeles. (USA)

■ 359 Photograph from an editorial feature in the magazine *Décoration Internationale*. (FRA)

■ 358 «Zwei Rosen» – Als Eigenwerbung des Photographen Dave Holt, Los Angeles, verwendete Aufnahme. (USA)

■ 359 Aufnahme aus einem redaktionellen Beitrag in der Zeitschrift *Décoration Internationale*. (FRA)

■ 358 «Deux Roses» – photo autopromotionnelle du photographe Dave Holt de Los Angeles. (USA)

■ 359 Photo illustrant un article paru dans le magazine spécialisé *Décoration Internationale*. (FRA)

PHOTOGRAPHER:
DAVE HOLT
PUBLISHER:
DAVE HOLT EDITIONS
ART DIRECTOR:
DAVE HOLT
DESIGNER:
FRED KIDDER
◄■ 358

PHOTOGRAPHER:
NICOLAS BRUANT
PUBLISHER:
DÉCORATION INTERNATIONALE
ART DIRECTOR:
HENRI LATZARUS
■ 359

PHOTOGRAPHER:
BETH GALTON
CLIENT:
BETH GALTON
ART DIRECTOR:
DAVID BENDER
DESIGNER:
DAVID BENDER
AGENCY:
JANKLOW, BENDER
■ 360

■ 360 Shot taken by New
York photographer Beth Galton, used for self-promotional purposes. (USA)

■ 360 Als Eigenwerbung
verwendete Aufnahme der
New Yorker Photographin
Beth Galton. (USA)

■ 360 Photo que la photo-
graphe new-yorkaise Beth
Galton utilise pour sa promotion. (USA)

PHOTOGRAPHER:
JAN OSWALD
PUBLISHER:
PORTAL PUBLICATIONS LTD.
ART DIRECTOR:
JAN OSWALD
DESIGNER:
BETTE TRONO
AGENCY:
JAN OSWALD PHOTOGRAPHY
■ 361

■ 361 Personal study by
photographer Jan Oswald,
who uses it as advertising
for his photo studio. (USA)

■ 361 Persönliche Studie des
Photographen Jan Oswald,
die er als Werbung für sein
Photostudio benutzt. (USA)

■ 361 Etude personnelle du
photographe Jan Oswald,
que l'on retrouve dans la
publicité directe. (USA)

PHOTOGRAPHER:
ROBERT MAPPLETHORPE
AGENCY:
ART + COMMERCE
■ 362-365

■ 362-365 Still lives with flowers, vases and bowles - shots taken by New York photographer Robert Mapplethorpe. (USA)

■ 362-365 Stilleben mit Blumen und Gefässen - Aufnahmen des New Yorker Photographen Robert Mapplethorpe. (USA)

■ 362-365 Natures mortes avec fleurs, coupes et vases - photos du photographe new-yorkais Robert Mapplethorpe. (USA)

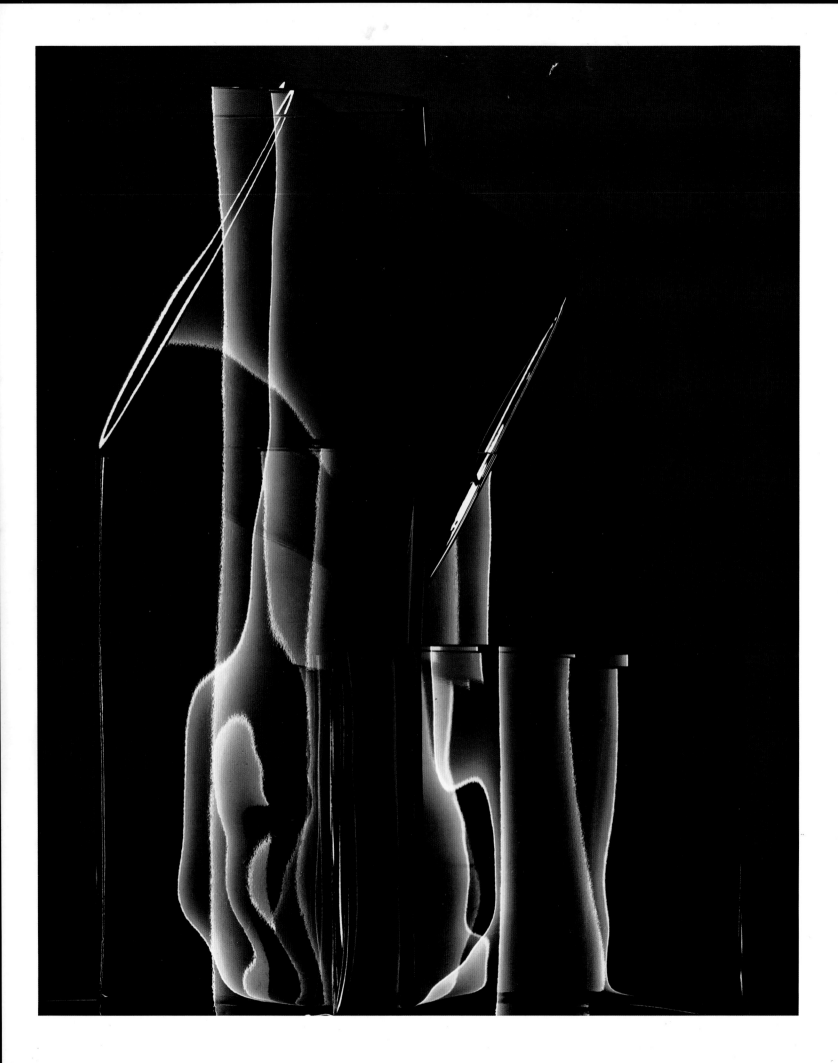

■ 367 The *Iittala Glass* articles, fashioned by contemporary designers, were photographed in an unconventional manner by Hans Hansen for the 1987 calendar for the *Dibbern Collection*. (GER)

■ 368 "The tulips have almost faded" is the title of this still life by photographer Hervé Tenot. (FRA)

■ 367 Die von zeitgenössischen Designern entworfenen *Iittala-Glas*-Artikel wurden von Hans Hansen für den Kalender 1987 der *Dibbern Collection* auf unkonventionelle Weise photographiert. (GER)

■ 368 «Die Tulpen sind bald verblüht» ist der Titel dieses Stillebens des Photographen Hervé Tenot. (FRA)

■ 367 Les créations en verre *Iittala* dues à des designers contemporains ont été photographiées de manière peu conventionnelle par Hans Hansen pour le calendrier 1987 de la *Dibbern Collection* en noir et blanc. (GER)

■ 368 «Les tulipes sont bientôt fanées», tel est le titre choisi ici par le photographe Hervé Tenot. (FRA)

PHOTOGRAPHER:
HANS HANSEN
CLIENT:
DIBBERN COLLECTION
ART DIRECTOR:
RANDOLPH NOLTE
AGENCY:
RANDOLPH NOLTE
◀■ 367

PHOTOGRAPHER:
HERVÉ TENOT
CLIENT:
HERVÉ TENOT
ART DIRECTOR:
HERVÉ TENOT
■ 368

PHOTOGRAPHER:
LOUIS WALLACH
CLIENT:
LOUIS WALLACH
PHOTOGRAPHY
ART DIRECTOR:
LOUIS WALLACH
■ 369

■ 369 Photograph for self-promotional purposes by Louis Wallach of New York. (USA)

■ 370 Personal study by London photographer Julian Nieman entitled "Leaf and Rainbow Drop". (GBR)

■ 369 Als Eigenwerbung verwendete Aufnahme von Louis Wallach, New York. (USA)

■ 370 Persönliche Studie des Londoner Photographen Julian Nieman mit dem Titel «Blatt und Regentropfen». (GBR)

■ 369 Photo du New-Yorkais Louis Wallach utilisée pour la promotion de cet artiste. (USA)

■ 370 Etude personnelle du photographe londonien Julian Nieman, qu'il a intitulée «Feuille et goutte de pluie». (GBR)

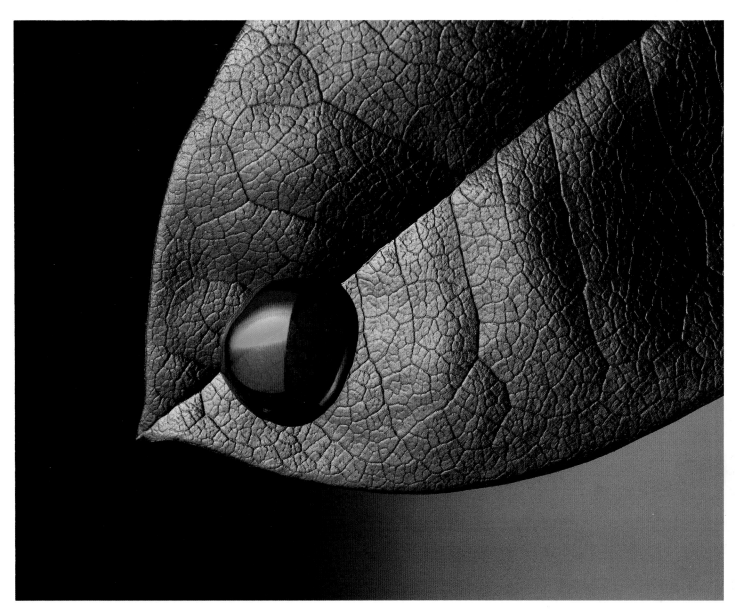

PHOTOGRAPHER:
JULIAN NIEMAN
CLIENT:
JULIAN NIEMAN
ART DIRECTOR:
JULIAN NIEMAN
■ 370

PHOTOGRAPHER:
CARIN KRASNER
ART DIRECTOR:
CARIN KRASNER
■ 371

■ 371 "Nantucket" (popular holiday island on the coast of Massachusetts) is the title of this still life by photographer Carin Krasner, Chicago. (USA)

■ 371 «Nantucket» (beliebte Ferieninsel vor der Küste Massachusetts) ist der Titel dieses Stillebens der Photographin Carin Krasner, Chicago. (USA)

■ 371 «Nantucket» (une île du Massachusetts prisée des vacanciers): c'est le titre donné à cette nature morte par la photographe Carin Krasner de Chicago. (USA)

FOOD

CUISINE

LEBENSMITTEL

CUISINE

PHOTOGRAPHER:
CARIN KRASNER
ART DIRECTOR:
CARIN KRASNER
■ 372

PHOTOGRAPHER:
SUSAN J. FRIEDMAN
CLIENT:
FRIEDMAN PHOTOGRAPHY
ART DIRECTOR:
SUSAN J. FRIEDMAN
STUDIO:
FRIEDMAN PHOTOGRAPHY
►■ 373

■ 372 "Still Life in the Afternoon" is the title of this photograph by Carin Krasner. (USA)

■ 373 Shot used as self-promotion by photographer Susan
J. Friedman of Chicago. (USA)

■ 372 «Stilleben am Nachmittag» ist der Titel dieser Aufnahme von Carin Krasner. (USA)

■ 373 Als Eigenwerbung verwendete Aufnahme der Photographin Susan J. Friedman, Chicago. (USA)

■ 372 «Nature morte l'après-midi», c'est le titre que Carin
Krasner donne à cette photo. (USA)

■ 373 Photo autopromotionnelle de la photographe Susan
J. Friedman de Chicago. (USA)

PHOTOGRAPHER:
TERRY HEFFERNAN
CLIENT:
WOLFER PRINTING CO.
ART DIRECTOR:
KIMBERLEE KESWICK/
GRETCHEN GOLDIE
DESIGNER:
KIMBERLEE KESWICK/
GRETCHEN GOLDIE
■ 374, 375

PHOTOGRAPHER:
ALF DIETRICH
CLIENT:
MIGROS GENOSSENSCHAFTSBUND
ART DIRECTOR:
THOMAS BOLLIGER
AGENCY:
BBWH
►■ 376

■ 374, 375 Full-page photographs taken by Terry Heffernan for an advertising brochure for *Wolfer* printers. They chose foodstuffs to prove their skills because with this theme a natural and also an appetizing presentation plays a major role. (USA)

■ 376 From an advertisement for *Migros* coffee. The slogan, roughly translated, is "All's well that smells well". (SWI)

■ 374, 375 Aufnahmen aus einer Werbebroschüre für die Druckerei *Wolfer,* die Nahrungsmittel für besonders geeignet hielt, um ihr Können unter Beweis zu stellen, weil bei diesem Thema eine naturgetreue und gleichzeitig appetitliche Darstellung eine grosse Rolle spielt. (USA)

■ 376 Ganzseitige Aufnahme aus einem Inserat für *Migros*-Kaffee. Der Slogan: Aroma gut, alles gut. (SWI)

■ 374, 375 Photos pleine page pour une brochure de l'imprimerie *Wolfer.* L'imprimeur a choisi des sujets alimentaires, estimant que leur reproduction donnait une bonne idée de la qualité de l'impression, vu que le lecteur s'attend à une représentation très réaliste qui le mette en appétit. (USA)

■ 376 Photo pleine page illustrant une annonce pour le café *Migros.* Le slogan: l'arôme d'un café authentique. (SWI)

PHOTOGRAPHER:
SUSAN J. FRIEDMAN
CLIENT:
FRIEDMAN PHOTOGRAPHY
ART DIRECTOR:
SUSAN J. FRIEDMAN
STUDIO:
FRIEDMAN PHOTOGRAPHY
■ 377

PHOTOGRAPHER:
BARRY SCHEIN
■ 378

■ 377 Photographer Susan J. Friedman of Chicago uses this photograph as self promotion. (USA)

■ 378 Unpublished photograph taken by Barry Schein of New York which he uses for self-promotional purposes. (USA)

■ 377 Als Eigenwerbung verwendete Aufnahme der Photographin Susan J. Friedman, Chicago. (USA)

■ 378 Unveröffentlichte Aufnahme des Photographen Barry Schein, New York, als Eigenwerbung verwendet. (USA)

■ 377 Sujet utilisé par la photographe Susan J. Friedman de Chicago pour sa promotion. (USA)

■ 378 Photo inédite du photographe Barry Schein de New York, qu'il utilise pour sa promotion. (USA)

PHOTOGRAPHER:
HIROYUKI YAMAMOTO
ART DIRECTOR:
HIROYUKI YAMAMOTO
DESIGNER:
HIROYUKI YAMAMOTO
■ 379

PHOTOGRAPHER:
JAIME MALÉ
ART DIRECTOR:
JAIME MALÉ
►■ 380

■ 379 Photographer Hiroyuki Yamamoto of Tokyo took this shot for his own self promotion. (JPN)

■ 380 Still life, reminiscent of an old painting. Photographer Jaime Malé works entirely without any retouching. (SPA)

■ 381-383 Photographs from a brochure for *Alex Brands,* a company that delivers firm's canteens and large kitchens with finished, ready-to-eat salads. (USA)

■ 379 Als Eigenwerbung verwendete Aufnahme des Photographen Hiroyuki Yamamoto, Tokio. (JPN)

■ 380 An ein altes Gemälde erinnerndes Stilleben des Photographen Jaime Malé, der ohne Retuschen arbeitet. (SPA)

■ 381-383 Aufnahmen für eine Firmenbroschüre von *Alex Brands,* ein Unternehmen, das Kantinen, Grossküchen usw. mit fertigen Salaten beliefert. (USA)

■ 379 Photo que le photographe Hiroyuki Yamamoto de Tokyo utilise pour sa publicité personnelle. (JPN)

■ 380 Nature morte du photographe Jaime Malé. Sans aucune retouche, elle évoque un tableau ancien. (SPA)

■ 381-383 D'une brochure de présentation d'*Alex Brands,* entreprise spécialisée dans la livraison de salades fraîches aux cantines, cuisines des collectivités, etc. (USA)

PHOTOGRAPHER:
George Monserrat
CLIENT:
Alex Brands, Inc.
ART DIRECTOR:
Kimberly Baer
DESIGNER:
Barbara Cooper
AGENCY:
Kimberly Baer Design
▼■ 381–383

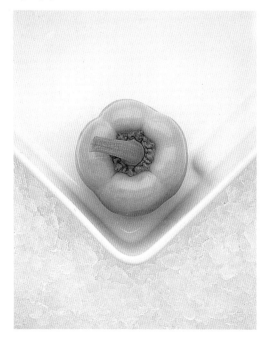

PHOTOGRAPHER:
PAUL FRANZ-MOORE
CLIENT:
PAUL FRANZ-MOORE
ART DIRECTOR:
PAUL FRANZ-MOORE
FOOD STYLIST:
AMY NATHAN
◄■ 384

PHOTOGRAPHER:
RODNEY RASCONA
CLIENT:
RASCONA STUDIO
ART DIRECTOR:
RODNEY RASCONA
■ 385, 386

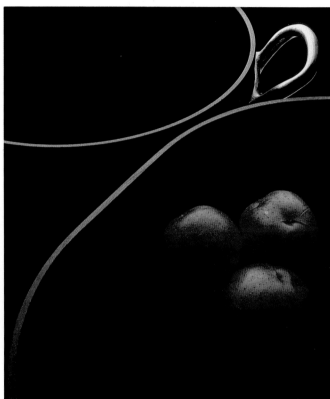

■ 384 This photograph was part of a series on "Offerings". It was used as a full-page, self-promotional ad in the special edition of *Photo Metro* magazine for the 1987 AIGA conference held in San Francisco. (USA)

■ 385, 386 "Curvilinear" and "Classic Black" are the titles of these photographs taken by Rodney Rascona for use as self promotion. (USA)

■ 384 Diese Aufnahme stammt aus einer Serie über Spezialitäten. Sie wurde in einer Spezialausgabe der Zeitschrift *Photo Metro* als ganzseitiges Inserat zur Eigenwerbung der AIGA Konferenz 1987 in San Francisco verwendet. (USA)

■ 385, 386 «Mit vielen Rundungen» und «Klassisches Schwarz» sind die Titel dieser für Eigenwerbung verwendeten Aufnahmen des Photographen Rodney Rascona. (USA)

■ 384 D'une série d'«Offres spéciales», cette photo a été utilisée comme annonce autopromotionnelle dans l'édition spéciale du magazine *Photo Metro* publiée à l'occasion de la conférence 1987 de l'AIGA à San Francisco. (USA)

■ 385, 386 «Curviligne», «Noir classique» – c'est ainsi que le photographe Rodney Rascona intitule ces photos employées dans sa promotion personnellé. (USA)

PHOTOGRAPHER:
Chris Collins
CLIENT:
Chris Collins
ART DIRECTOR:
Chris Collins
DESIGNER:
Fiorentino, Leibe Associates
■ 387

■ 387 Photograph used for self-promotional purposes, taken by Chris Collins of New York. (USA)

■ 388 From a feature in the German *Vogue* on fruits entitled "Fruit-Bar". (GER)

■ 389 Salmon is the subject of a feature in the German *Vogue* to which this full-page photograph belongs. (GER)

■ 387 Als Eigenwerbung verwendete Aufnahme des New Yorker Photographen Chris Collins. (USA)

■ 388 Photographie zu einem Artikel über Obst in der deutschen *Vogue* unter dem Titel «Frucht-Bar». (GER)

■ 389 Lachs ist das Thema des Beitrags in der deutschen *Vogue*, zu dem diese ganzseitige Aufnahme gehört. (GER)

■ 387 Photo de Chris Collins, de New York, que l'artiste utilise pour sa publicité. (USA)

■ 388 Photo illustrant un article de l'édition allemande de *Vogue* consacré aux fruits («Bar aux fruits»). (GER)

■ 389 Photo pleine page illustrant un article que l'édition allemande de *Vogue* consacre au saumon. (GER)

PHOTOGRAPHER:
MICHAEL SOMOROFF
CLIENT:
DEUTSCHE VOGUE
PUBLISHER:
CONDÉ NAST VERLAG GMBH
ART DIRECTOR:
ANGELICA BLECHSCHMIDT
■ 388

PHOTOGRAPHER:
CHRISTIAN VON ALVENSLEBEN
CLIENT:
DEUTSCHE VOGUE
PUBLISHER:
CONDÉ NAST VERLAG GMBH
ART DIRECTOR:
ANGELICA BLECHSCHMIDT
■ 389

PHOTOGRAPHER:
MICHAEL GEIGER
◀■ 390

PHOTOGRAPHER:
RICK GAYLE
CLIENT:
LASERSCAN
DESIGNER:
MIKE PARSONS
■ 391

■ 390 "Konstruction with Pears" is the title of this photograph by Michael Geiger (USA) which appeared in an article in *Camera International* in connection with the exhibition "Fifty Years of Color Photography 1936–1986" – a part of Photokina 1986. (FRA)

■ 391 Photographs used as advertising for the print lithographers *Laserscan.* (USA)

■ 390 «Konstruktion mit Birnen» ist der Titel dieser Aufnahme von Michael Geiger (USA), veröffentlicht in einem Artikel in *Camera International* über die Ausstellung «Fünfzig Jahre Farbphotographie 1936–1986»; die ein Teil der Photokina 1986 war. (FRA)

■ 391 Als Werbung für die Lithographenanstalt *Laserscan* verwendete Aufnahme. (USA)

■ 390 «Construction aux poires» – photo de Michael Geiger (Etats-Unis) publiée dans un article de *Camera International* qui rend compte de l'exposition «50 ans de photographie en couleurs 1936–1986» organisée dans le cadre de la Photokina 1986. (FRA)

■ 391 Photo utilisée pour la publicité de l'atelier de lithographie *Laserscan.* (USA)

PHOTOGRAPHER:
MICHAEL LAMOTTE
PUBLISHER:
ADWEEK
ART DIRECTOR:
MICHAEL LAMOTTE
STUDIO:
MICHAEL LAMOTTE STUDIOS, INC.
■ 392, 393

■ 392, 393 These self promotion shots by Michael Lamotte were also published in *Adweek*. This photographer sees food as an art form and his favorite challenge is to create images of diverse elements, unifying a great variety of objects and textures. Amy Nathan set up the arrangements. (USA)

■ 392, 393 Als Eigenwerbung des Photographen Michael Lamotte in *Adweek* veröffentlichte Aufnahmen. Kompositionen vieler Elemente der verschiedensten Formen und Strukturen gehören zu seinen Lieblingsthemen. Die Arrangements machte Amy Nathan. (USA)

■ 392, 393 Photos utilisées pour l'autopromotion du photographe Michael Lamotte et publiées dans *Adweek*. L'artiste affectionne les compositions multiformes réunissant des éléments de forme et de structure très diverse. Assemblages d'Amy Nathan. (USA)

PHOTOGRAPHER:
LOUIS WALLACH
CLIENT:
LOUIS WALLACH PHOTOGRAPHY
ART DIRECTOR:
LOUIS WALLACH
■ 394

■ 394 Photographer Louis Wallach of New York uses this photograph as self promotion. (USA)

■ 394 Als Eigenwerbung verwendete Aufnahme des Photographen Louis Wallach, New York. (USA)

■ 394 Photo réalisée par le photographe Louis Wallach de New York et qui lui sert d'autopromotion. (USA)

INDEX

INDEX

VERZEICHNIS

INDEX

SUBSCRIBE TO GRAPHIS: FOR USA AND CANADA

MAGAZINE	USA	CANADA
☐ GRAPHIS (One year/6 issues)	US$ 79.00	CDN$ 99.00
☐ 1987 Portfolio (Case holds six issues)	US$ 11.00	CDN$ 15.00

☐ Check enclosed
☐ Please bill me (My subscription will begin upon payment)
☐ Students may request a 40% discount by sending student ID.
IMPORTANT! PLEASE CHECK THE LANGUAGE VERSION DESIRED:
☐ ENGLISH   ☐ GERMAN   ☐ FRENCH
Subscription fees include postage to any part of the world.
Surcharge of US$ 16.00 (CDN$ 21.00) for Airmail.

NAME

TITLE

COMPANY

ADDRESS

CITY

STATE/PROV.   POSTAL CODE

COUNTRY

PROFESSION

SIGNATURE   DATE

Please send coupon and make check payable to:
GRAPHIS US, INC., 141 LEXINGTON AVENUE, NEW YORK, NY 10016, USA.
Guarantee: You may cancel your subscription at any time and receive a full refund on all
unmailed copies. Please allow 6–8 weeks for delivery of first issue.

REQUEST FOR CALL FOR ENTRIES
Please put me on your "Call for Entries" list for the following title(s).
Please check the appropriate box(es).
☐ GRAPHIS PHOTO   ☐ GRAPHIS POSTER   ☐ GRAPHIS DESIGN
☐ GRAPHIS PACKAGING   ☐ GRAPHIS DIAGRAM   ☐ GRAPHIS ANNUAL REPORTS
By submitting material to any of the titles listed above, I will automatically qualify for a
25% discount toward the purchase of the title.   GP 88

SUBSCRIBE TO GRAPHIS: FOR EUROPE AND THE WORLD

MAGAZINE	BRD	WORLD	U.K.
☐ GRAPHIS (One year/6 issues)	DM 146,-	SFr. 118.-	£ 45.00
☐ 1987 Portfolio (Case holds six issues)	DM 24.-	SFr. 19.-	£ 8.00

☐ Check enclosed (for Europe, please make SFr.-checks
   payable to a Swiss bank)
☐ Please bill me (My subscription will begin upon payment)
☐ Students may request a 40% discount by sending student ID.
IMPORTANT! PLEASE CHECK THE LANGUAGE VERSION DESIRED:
☐ ENGLISH   ☐ GERMAN   ☐ FRENCH
Subscription fees include postage to any part of the world. Latin America and India-
Registered Mail: Add SFr. 12.- Surcharge of SFr. 25.- (£10.00) for Airmail.

NAME

TITLE

COMPANY

ADDRESS

CITY   POSTAL CODE

COUNTRY

PROFESSION

SIGNATURE   DATE

Please send coupon and make check payable to:
GRAPHIS PRESS CORP, DUFOURSTRASSE 107, CH-8008 ZÜRICH, SWITZERLAND
Guarantee: You may cancel your subscription at any time and receive a full refund on all
unmailed copies. Please allow 6–8 weeks for delivery of first issue.

REQUEST FOR CALL FOR ENTRIES
Please put me on your "Call for Entries" list for the following title(s).
Please check the appropriate box(es).
☐ GRAPHIS PHOTO   ☐ GRAPHIS POSTER   ☐ GRAPHIS DESIGN
☐ GRAPHIS PACKAGING   ☐ GRAPHIS DIAGRAM   ☐ GRAPHIS ANNUAL REPORTS
By submitting material to any of the titles listed above, I will automatically qualify for a
25% discount toward the purchase of the title.   GP 88

BOOK ORDER FORM: FOR USA AND CANADA

ORDER YOUR GRAPHIS ANNUALS NOW!

BOOKS	USA	CANADA
☐ Graphis Poster 88	US$ 59.50	CDN$ 79.50
☐ Graphis Design Annual 87/88	US$ 59.50	CDN$ 79.50
☐ GRAPHIS Photo 88	US$ 59.50	CDN$ 79.50
☐ Graphis Diagram 88	US$ 59.50	CDN$ 79.50
☐ Graphis Annual Reports	US$ 59.50	CDN$ 79.50
☐ Photographis 86	US$ 59.50	CDN$ 79.50
☐ Graphis Posters 86	US$ 59.50	CDN$ 79.50
☐ 42 Years of Graphis Covers	US$ 49.50	CDN$ 60.00

☐ Check enclosed
☐ Please bill me (Mailing costs in addition to above book price will be charged)

NAME

TITLE

COMPANY

ADDRESS

CITY/STATE/PROV.

POSTAL CODE   COUNTRY

PROFESSION

SIGNATURE   DATE

Please send coupon and make check payable to:
GRAPHIS US, INC., 141 LEXINGTON AVENUE, NEW YORK, NY 10016, USA.

REQUEST FOR CALL FOR ENTRIES
Please put me on your "Call for Entries" list for the following title(s).
Please check the appropriate box(es).
☐ GRAPHIS PHOTO   ☐ GRAPHIS POSTER   ☐ GRAPHIS DESIGN
☐ GRAPHIS PACKAGING   ☐ GRAPHIS DIAGRAM   ☐ GRAPHIS ANNUAL REPORTS
By submitting material to any of the titles listed above, I will automatically qualify for a
25% discount toward the purchase of the title.   GP 88

BOOK ORDER FORM: FOR EUROPE AND THE WORLD

BOOKS	BRD	WORLD	U.K.
☐ Graphis Poster 88	DM 138,-	SFr. 112.-	£ 45.00
☐ Graphis Design Annual 87/88	DM 138,-	SFr. 112.-	£ 45.00
☐ Graphis Photo 88	DM 138,-	SFr. 112.-	£ 45.00
☐ Graphis Diagram	DM 138,-	SFr. 112.-	£ 45.00
☐ Graphis Annual Reports	DM 138,-	SFr. 112.-	£ 45.00
☐ Photographis 86	DM 138,-	SFr. 112.-	£ 45.00
☐ Graphis Posters 86	DM 129,-	SFr. 105.-	£ 42.00
☐ 42 Years of Graphis Covers	DM 98,-	SFr. 85.-	£ 35.00

☐ Check enclosed (For Europe, please make SFr. checks payable to a Swiss Bank)
☐ Amount paid into Graphis account at the Union Bank of Switzerland, Acct No 3620063
   in Zürich.
☐ Amount paid to Postal Cheque Account Zürich 80-23071-9 (Through your local post office)
☐ Please bill me (Mailing costs in addition to above book price will be charged)

NAME

TITLE

COMPANY

ADDRESS

CITY   POSTAL CODE

COUNTRY

PROFESSION

SIGNATURE   DATE

Please send coupon and make check payable to:
GRAPHIS PRESS CORP, DUFOURSTRASSE 107, CH-8008 ZÜRICH, SWITZERLAND

REQUEST FOR CALL FOR ENTRIES
Please put me on your "Call for Entries" list for the following title(s).
Please check the appropriate box(es).
☐ GRAPHIS PHOTO   ☐ GRAPHIS POSTER   ☐ GRAPHIS DESIGN
☐ GRAPHIS PACKAGING   ☐ GRAPHIS DIAGRAM   ☐ GRAPHIS ANNUAL REPORTS
By submitting material to any of the titles listed above, I will automatically qualify for a
25% discount toward the purchase of the title.   GP 88

GRAPHIS PRESS CORP.
DUFOURSTRASSE 107
CH-8008 ZÜRICH
SWITZERLAND

GRAPHIS U.S., INC.
141 LEXINGTON AVENUE
NEW YORK, NEW YORK 10016
U.S.A.

GRAPHIS PRESS CORP.
DUFOURSTRASSE 107
CH-8008 ZÜRICH
SWITZERLAND

GRAPHIS U.S., INC.
141 LEXINGTON AVENUE
NEW YORK, NEW YORK 10016
U.S.A.